CAREER READINESS AND PREPARATION CRITERIA IN UNDERGRADUATE DANCE DEGREE PROGRAMS

Kathleen E. Klein

Hamilton Books
A member of
The Rowman & Littlefield Publishing Group
Lanham · Boulder · New York · Toronto · Plymouth, UK

Copyright © 2009 by
Hamilton Books
4501 Forbes Boulevard
Suite 200
Lanham, Maryland 20706
Hamilton Books Acquisitions Department (301) 459-3366

Estover Road
Plymouth PL6 7PY
United Kingdom

Library of Congress Control Number: 2009934335
ISBN-13: 978-0-7618-4863-9 (paperback : alk. paper)
ISBN-10: 0-7618-4863-0 (paperback : alk. paper)
eISBN-13: 978-0-7618-4864-6
eISBN-10: 0-7618-4864-9

∞™ The paper used in this publication meets the minimum
requirements of American National Standard for Information
Sciences—Permanence of Paper for Printed Library Materials,
ANSI Z39.48-1992

Contents

Preface

The purpose of the research study was to examine the history and philosophy of certain very distinct dance degree programs. The dissertation is intended to serve as a resource to benefit faculty and administrators in American undergraduate- and graduate- level dance programs. The primary goal was to recognize emergent themes aimed at stronger outcomes for students seeking a career track in dance. Beginning with an overview of the historical development of dance and dance education in the United States, the study closely examined the current cultural, educational, and political structures, functions, and mechanisms that influence prevailing public views of this art form in mainstream American life.

These views frame fundamental topics for the field of postsecondary dance education regarding curriculum, instruction, and definitions of professional career possibilities. These topics and their subtopics contributed to the formulation of qualitative questions, which were devised to document perceptions, attitudes, opinions, and practices of the participants in the study. The participants consisted of faculty at eight targeted postsecondary institutions.

A variety of instrumentation was employed in order to collect and record pertinent data. These included guided interviews and follow-up questions for selected individuals. Additional focused studies required oral interviews in person or via phone. As themes and patterns emerged, creative data displays were developed in order to facilitate systemic analysis. The findings of this research were reported in an objective voice, presenting and preserving the quantitative data gathered from the participants' words. The analysis and interpretation of this research was filtered through this researcher's specific lens, with the intention of discovering the effective principles and practices that the institutions utilize to impact individual students, the profession, and the dance community at large. It is further hoped that this study will serve as a catalyst for interacademic dialogue in order to strengthen and advocate for the integrity and position of dance education in American colleges and universities.

Acknowledgments

This book represents my research and is the culmination of my study on dance in higher education. I entered the PhD program at Lynn University with trepidation—unsure that I would ever complete all the requirements necessary for the degree, primarily due to other commitments with my family and business. I realized that if I was to complete the program, I would have to take "it one step at a time." Throughout the journey of completing the doctoral degree, many people assisted me, including every course and every person, whether faculty, staff, colleagues, study participants, family, or members of the research community.

Throughout my time at this university, I was constantly encouraged by the faculty, staff, and students of the PhD program. I wish to express my gratitude to Dr. William J. Leary, Dr. Richard Cohen, and Dr. Leah Kinniburgh for their guidance, instruction, and friendship. Thank you to Dr. Robert De Young for his expertise in working with NVivo qualitative software. Thank you also to the Lynn University Ross College of Education for providing an educational structure and housing faculty and staff dedicated to teaching and learning.

Thank you to Dr. Lloyd Mims, who afforded me precious time from my daily work schedule to prepare my book.

Thank you to my participants. Without you, this study could not have been done. Thank you for giving me your time, trust, and words.

I wish to extend a special thanks to my sister, Dr. Anne Rakip, who has always been my mentor, my editor, and my best friend.

Finally, I would like to thank my husband, Demetrius, my children Nicholas and Gabriel, my mother, Ruth, and my friends Mark and Paula for allowing me to pursue my academic endeavors. Without the support, encouragement, understanding, and respect you gave me, I could not have completed this work.

Thank you all. May God's presence always fill your lives.

Chapter One

Introduction to the Study

Background

Traditional Western understandings and discussions about the role of artistic expression frequently focus on and describe the relationship of art to recorded history. Artistic expression and its relationship to art attest to its necessity and importance to people, community, culture, spirituality, and religion. Within that context, there also historically exists a wide range of diverse tastes and opinions pertaining to the purpose and function of art (Hodes 1998).

For example, a lecturer, a wealthy philanthropist, a foundation grant maker, or a writer for a newspaper's society page may have a tendency to believe that "serious art" must be attractive, marvelous, expensive, or sophisticated. A fundamentalist Christian may claim that art is a threat to morality, gender, and so-called traditional family values (Fischer 1988). Art, as practiced by socially conscious activists who are dedicated to community-based work, can be discovered in such diverse settings as youth at risk, people with disabilities, people with mental illness and in prisons, hospitals, and nursing homes (Cleveland 2000). There are contemporary bohemian icons represented as characters in the Broadway musical *Rent*, who exuberantly reject the pronouncement that art is the dying victim of an American culture of corporate greed, homogenization, and politicization (Larson 1997). Cynically, the disillusioned or jaded observer of all these scenes might simply recall the comment of Andy Warhol (1928–1987) whose definition of art was "anything you can get away with" (Bockris 1997, 49).

Each perspective is indicative of the power of the arts as a vehicle to express the inner thoughts and feelings of individuals or communities through active external communication. The enormous impact and importance of artistic expression for individuals and society as a whole reflect what is generally accepted and considered as an ancient need for humans to connect with others and become known.

> From the earliest times, humans have communicated their most profound thoughts and deepest feelings through music, dance, drama, and art . . . [The arts are] the means by which we make sense of the world and our individual and collective experiences in it. They help us appreciate our rich cultural heritage in the United States and the cultures of others throughout the world (*Learning Through the Arts: A Guide to the National Endowment for the Arts* 2002, 43).

In addition to linking mysterious and spiritual impulses, art in prehistoric times was also essential to survival—as critical as food, water, sleep, shelter, sex, and worship (Anderson 1977). From the scraping out of maps in the form of cave paintings to each evening's reenactments around a fire of the day's hunt, our earliest ancestors already were employing the tools of artistic expression in order to make meaning of their lives. They were simultaneously, consciously, and actively discovering expressive tools to transform such everyday experiences into conveyable forms that could teach through recreating an experience. Large life-essential, functional truths of everyday living were communicated with deliberate intention (Ellfeldt 1976). However, we now realize that the arts also have survived because humans discovered that very personal and subtle truths could also be communicated—in fact, imparted—when given aesthetic form (Brockett 2003).

Dance is just one art form, among many, that has always played a major role in forming identity and facilitating communication among people, cultures, and countries (Land 2000). In fact, in the opinion of dance theoretician Rudolph Laban (1879–1958), the process of creation in many art forms is inherently dependent upon the specific mechanics of human movement and thus is a common denominator interrelating the disciplines (Hanna 1999). Speaking specifically of the visual artist, Laban (1971) states,

> The movements he has used in drawing, painting, or modeling have given character to his creations, and they remain fixed in the still-

visible strokes of his pencil, brush, or chisel. The activity of his mind
is revealed in the form he has given to his material (1971, 9).

Visual and aural products result from the effort expended in combining of movement and energy (Cohen 2002).

For many years in American society, the characteristics present in
the act of pure dance—self-expression, physical fitness, intellectual stimu-
lation, creative problem solving, and enjoyable group interaction—were
not recognized for the benefits that today are understood to be possible
for individuals or entire communities. This misperception largely ordained the historic opposition to dance in America over a period of nearly
four centuries, from the Puritans to the present (Wagner 1997).

In 1983, Howard Gardner's groundbreaking research and writing
(*Frames of Mind*) regarding the seven intelligences catalyzed a major
shift in thinking pertaining to the musical, visual-spatial, and body-ki-
nesthetic aspects of learning. Based upon the premise that the creative
process of the artist depends upon the principles and practices of organizing compositional elements, educators began to reconsider the necessity for aesthetic education in developing a child's capacity for critical
thinking. Integration of the arts into traditional curriculum and instruction regained momentum in K–12 classrooms as well as in higher education. Because dance develops particular acuity in rhythm, music, pattern, linear design, and cause-effect, movement experiences gained
acceptance and contributed to the development of new instructional approaches in elementary, middle, and high schools (Crawford 1987).

The validity of dance programs in American colleges and universities is an issue significant to educational leadership. Therefore, this investigative study addresses the following research question:

> *What are the effective principles and practices that exist in*
> *effective university level dance programs that sufficiently*
> *prepare students for career paths in dance?*

In order for the research question to be clearly delineated as well as
to have completeness, it is necessary to have a framework for understanding the progression through history of the worldviews that both
value and oppose dance. Therefore, this research study begins with an
overview of the evolution of dance.

Dance in Identity Formation of Individuals and Societies

Cultural Dance Worldviews

Like a modern-day screenwriter, this following Old Testament historian captures the catalytic power of dance to simultaneously ignite both emotional and spiritual expression:

> Saul was told that David was in Naioth in Ramah, so he sent some men to arrest him. They saw the group of prophets dancing and shouting, with Samuel as their leader. Then the spirit of God took control of Saul's men and they also began to dance and shout. When Saul heard of this, he sent more messengers, and they also began to dance and shout . . . As he [Saul] was going there, the spirit of God took control of him also, and he danced and shouted all the way to Naioth. He took off his clothes and danced and shouted in Samuel's presence (1 Samuel 19:19-24, translation, Good News Bible).

A history of dance, like an overview of art in any of its manifestations—visual, aural, or kinetic—is inevitably a study of the development, metamorphosis, and transformation of human creative activities that parallel changes in society (Smith-Autard 1994). In such inquiries, we discover the relationships between the art forms and identity formation in individuals and society. However, each art discipline uniquely provides its own metaphoric meanings that enable the creator to code information, ideas, or feelings. The recipient of the created product—the reader, viewer, or individual members of a group of recipients called an audience—learns and can "translate" the language of the art form. In doing so, one viscerally experiences and interprets the intention of the creator's expression (Ellfeldt 1976).

Unlike a dancer, the painter or graphic artist employs acrylics, oils, charcoal, and pencil to transmit a vision singularly held in that creator's mind's eye (Knobler 1971). This image is placed on a canvas, and the viewer is left alone to interpret. Or for the sculptor, clay must be molded, carved, and shaped to display an object of texture, color, and three dimensions revealing and manifesting the vision of its maker and again creating a distinctly personal response in the observer. In both instances, the visual art exists beyond the fixed time frame of its initial creation. However, the intended meaning or the interpretation of the work might endure or could change in response to the evolution of cultural sensibilities over time (Crawford 1987).

Also unlike dance, in literature, a timeless and enduring relationship between writer and reader can afford, perhaps, the most personal, private, and enigmatic of all the artistic exchanges. Literary arts shape language, constructing and deconstructing words into the forms of prose or poetry. Mental images are created in the mind of the reader, ranging from very abstract to highly specific linear narratives yet within each reader a unique interpretation and meaning is actualized at an individual level (Barranger 1994).

Additionally, through literature, certain works enter society and become incorporated into a shared vocabulary of the cultural lexicon and conscience as demonstrated in the repeated readings by entire American generations of works such as *The Legend of Sleepy Hollow, The Adventures of Huckleberry Finn, Catcher in the Rye, To Kill a Mockingbird*, as well as the Hardy Boys, Nancy Drew, and the Harry Potter series. An author's words can become even more accessible also via the power of the mass media such as in Maya Angelou's (1992) poem "On the Pulse of Morning" created for President Bill Clinton's 1993 inauguration. The line "A rock, a river, a tree hosts to species long since departed . . ." might never have reached and affected an audience of millions had it not been actually delivered live and beamed via television and radio into every living room tuned to the event. Over thirty years prior, for newly elected presidential candidate John F. Kennedy (1961) spoke the phrase, "Ask not what your country can do for you, but what you can do for your country." These words became not only viscerally etched with personal application into the minds of millions but also came to represent a major philosophical benchmark in American political history. Even the marketing and advertising industries have originated and disseminated many contemporary slogans and phrases such as "Mm, mm, good!" "When it rains it pours," "Ka-ching!" and "Where's the beef?" Originated by talented copywriters, these miniatures of meaning occupy permanent iconic status in the vernacular of American popular culture (Crawford 1987).

While dance, similar to literary arts, can also present a snapshot of zeitgeist (spirit of the times), aural artistic expression accomplishes the same ends (Pomer 2002). Through tonal inflections used in recitation by a speaker, subtext—what is suggested "between the lines"—deepens the meaning of the printed word. Through the event of theater, an entire ensemble of actors can, through the mutually agreed upon willing suspension of disbelief on the parts of both performers and audience, create a living linear reality solely from the text—the instructions—in a script (Cohen 2002). Music—vocal, choral, and instrumental—further transform and heighten both language and feeling through many sophisticated techniques of manipulating, expanding, and compressing time. Opera endeavors, through integrating these interrelated disciplines, to communicate a story in a process often considered to be one of the most ambitious and complex of all art forms (Brockett 2003, 416).

Dance artists participate in what many believe is the strongest form of human expression and communication. Radically dissimilar to the aforementioned art forms, there have been myriad definitions of this kinetic art form throughout history. Invariably, however, any given definition will include two essential components: the body and movement. No other form of art requires that these two elements combine in some form in order for intentional expression to occur (Minton 2003).

Fundamentally, there are numerous daily and seemingly ordinary accomplishments that involve many of the same considerations, choices, and tasks inherent in dance. These could include the traditionally challenging act of parallel parking; the common courtesy and improvisational dexterity required to physically negotiate around dozens of other human bodies along the same crowded sidewalk; even the process of negotiating weight, balance, speed, coordination, function, and aesthetic taste while maneuvering people and objects through narrow spatial paths during the sometimes innocuous, sometimes daunting assignment of moving furniture into a new home (Brown 1975).

In a different context of meaning, variations of dance are also embodied in such occurrences as a wave of greeting or farewell at the airport, the shaking of hands following the signing of an international treaty or a baby's first steps. These physicalities hold, for the participants or the observers, deeply cherished meanings embodied in the specific emotional moment. The memories are often permanently captured and preciously fixed in time by the tools of the photographer or painter, creating enduring meaning for families and communities (Franklin 1996).

The human body, because of its ability to move freely, can give meaning to whatever movement it creates. As the sole vehicle of expression, the physical, intellectual, emotional, and spiritual powers of the body become evident. In dance, the holistic blending of all the senses with physicality and spirituality transforms the work beyond its canvas—in itself totally human (Minton 2003).

Not unlike different actors or singers interpreting the same text, characters, or musical notes, the soul of each individual dancer is inhabited in the singular uniqueness of each human body. Although future dancers may accurately replicate physical movements, capturing the precise soul and spirit of the original performance is never possible (Pomer 2002).

From ritual primitive forms, classical ballet, and contemporary dance, there has been, throughout dance history, a constant search for what is new, vital, and most appropriate to its time, place, and culture. The emphasis in dance on achieving technical perfection—in fact, virtuosity—mirrors society's ongoing pursuit of excellence and mandate to accomplish new and greater feats (Hodes 1998).

Through the intentional movement of the human body, dance can display a full spectrum of emotions or tell specific stories. In either purpose, dance can strengthen and refresh an individual and the audience. Dance is often a primary component of nonverbal communication in most societies: in religious worship, displays of power, rites of passage, courtship and dating, celebrations, and entertainment (Dimondstein 1971).

On a daily basis, dance is inherently social and reflective of a culture's views of life, including its preoccupations. One need only look within the sociological fabric of daily contemporary American cultural life to discover other movement-based American pastimes that derive their identities in significant ways from elements of dance: MTV rock videos; Las Vegas spectacles; Cirque de Soleil; martial arts; marching bands; synchronized swimming, equestrian and dolphin shows; the choreography of football plays; highly acrobatic and athletic high school and college pompom dance competitions; "aggressive" skateboarding, biking, and in-line skating; children's gymnastics programs; Olympic events such as figure skating, competitive diving or snow jumping; and the proliferation of Arthur Murray Dance Studios franchises. These wide-ranging social phenomena require such tasks as organizing space, creating patterns, defying gravity, or displaying of physical daring or virtuosity. However, there is a distinction between such feats and experiencing a deep level of spiritual, emotional, or aesthetic response to the body in motion. The experience of dance must ultimately examine the intimately personal nature of individual response to participation in this art form (Mirault 1998).

In any movement, the learner plans the movement based upon the action goal. For any movement-related activities, e.g., basketball or football, the goal of the movement is related to the outcome rather than the quality of the movement itself. From this perspective, dance as movement is based on a different set of criteria for successful performance. Not only is the successful technical execution of a movement considered but also how the movement is performed in terms of space, time, and energy. Dance movement is internally organized. The outcome is tied to the individuality of the performer. It is this uniqueness that makes dance an aesthetic experience. The individual not only shapes the movement but also makes aesthetic choices about how to use movement qualities to create dynamic and articulate movement that expresses the inner organization and intent of the performer (Wood and Gillis-Kruman 1991, 75).

Communication is a basic form of belonging and membership in the family of man. In fact, since belonging is a basic human need, the ability to communicate is essential (Maslow 1934). Communication is expressed by both verbal and nonverbal means. Yet, as applied to all of the arts, including dance, there is an apparent paradox of thought in America in the twenty-first century:

Think about it: Why do many of the smartest, most talented, most demanding people work like maniacs in fields that won't make them wealthy or secure? What is it about the arts that draws and satisfies so many of the best and brightest people who could be high achievers in more lucrative professions? What is it about art that has kept it near the top of the human priority list for the last twenty-thousand years until its slippage in recent generations? Artists are not foolish; they are not old-fashioned; they're onto something (Booth 1997, 15).

As Booth suggests, a conflict is inherent between socially constructed goals and artistic pursuit. Success in a modern capitalist society is often measured by fiduciary soundness, and yet art and its creation have served to touch humanity, surviving and thriving with conflict as its crux and wealth creation always out of reach (Booth 1997).

Purpose of the Study

The purpose of this study was to describe the history and philosophy of certain very distinct postsecondary dance degree programs and to examine them for the effective principles and practices that they utilize to impact individual students, the profession, and the dance community at large. The study assessed these programs with the end goal of recognizing criteria and standards that most successfully contribute to stronger outcomes for students seeking a career track in dance. The aim was to suggest themes that a variety of institutions might find useful or might adapt in order to improve or enhance the qualities of their own existing programs.

Only a few decades ago, dance programs were difficult to locate on college campuses. While colleges and universities typically required course work in the arts in order to satisfy minimum requirements for an undergraduate degree in any field, few offered actual degrees in dance or dance education. Those programs that could be identified were quietly tucked into theater or physical education departments. Today, degrees in dance are offered through dance departments at over three hundred colleges and universities scattered all over the United States (Hanna 1999).

Recently, some Christian colleges have also begun offering degrees in dance, often with a specialization in dance ministry. Dance within Christian-based curricula is considered by many to be an innovative, if not groundbreaking accomplishment, as the two were previously not considered compatible (Fischer 1988). For Christian students who previously wanted to pursue a degree in dance, the only recourse for locating a well-balanced program was to enroll in a secular university or to attend a Christian school while foregoing the possibility of majoring in dance.

However, uniform standards for college- and university-level programs in dance education have not been formulated. The 1994 position paper the *National Standards for Arts Education* represents the culmination of work conducted in the largest consensus development project on study of the arts at the K–12 level. It has been adopted or adapted in forty-seven states and supported by eighty national organizations. No similar professional position paper exists for the postsecondary level. Without a unified national set of standards to guide the articulation of goals and objectives within individual programs, the criteria that students and parents can use to distinguish strengths and weaknesses among prospective schools is understandably limited. By extension, how can students achieve discrimination in envisioning employment possibilities within a potential career path beyond graduation?

The Research Question

The research question that was investigated asked this:

*What are the effective principles and practices that exist
in effective university-level dance programs that sufficiently
prepare students for career paths in dance?*

Dance programs were defined in this study as dance education and dance performance (see operational definition of terms, p. 14). The research study examined eight very distinct existing postsecondary dance programs in the United States in order to discover the effective principles and practices in curriculum and instruction that can be attributed to successful employment for graduating students. It is hoped that the conclusions of this study will serve as a valid and valuable resource for colleges, universities, and many other communities of dance artists.

Topics explored in seeking answers to the research question grew out of discussions with working and retired professional dancers, high school students interested in pursuing professional or college-level dance training, parents, other doctoral students, arts advocates, dance professionals, and other employers in the related fields of the arts, education, and arts education.

These topics included current cultural, educational, and political constructs that influence prevailing public views of dance; the history of postsecondary dance programs; the importance of postsecondary dance programs to society; the roles of supportive home and community environments in preparing a student for enrollment in a postsecondary dance program; aptitudes and prerequisites necessary for acceptance and enrollment into postsecondary dance programs; how students use the degree; the qualifications and skill sets attractive to and desired by prospective employers of dance program graduates.

Definition of Terms

Certain dance-related concepts have been imbedded in the text of this study in order to educate the reader in the vernacular of the dance field. Other useful definitions are listed below in order to facilitate the reader's understanding of dance terminology within the context of this research.

- Body awareness (kinesthetic awareness)—the act of being aware of conscious movements of the body, parts of the body, or kinesthetic feelings in the body (Todd 1959).
- Classical Ballet—dance movement forms using traditional steps, body positioning and carriage originating before the twentieth century (Grant 1982).
- Choreographer—one who discovers movement and organizes it into dances (Minton 1997).
- Corps—a ballet term for a group of dancers that perform together (Hammond 1982).
- Creative Process—act of making or causing a work to come into existence (Hodes 1998).
- Modern Dance—a performance creative dance form created at the beginning of the twentieth century (Erkert 2003).
- Technique—the learning of movement skills; the ability to use specific methods to create a dance (Grant 1982).
- Dance—any type of human movement, from simple hand gestures by an individual to complex ballets requiring many performers (Horst 1979).
- Dance Education—the study of an art form that develops kinesthetic intelligence; teaches the values and skills of creativity, problem-solving, risk-taking, and higher-order thinking skills; offers a historical "window of civilization" and helps the student to develop understanding and respect through cultural studies of movement (Hanna 1999).
- Dance Performance—the study of an art form that aids in creating opportunities for self-expression and communication within the constraints of the medium of the body (Hanna 1999).

Limitations of the Study

The primary goal of the study was to identify commonalities for success attained by departments of dance or dance programs contained within postsecondary fine arts divisions without intending to suggest a recipe card system guaranteeing success. However, because today's economic climate dictates that tuition dollars, scholarship subsidies, and philanthropy be so competitively sought and awarded, it is incumbent to establish a framework and vocabulary that conveys an understanding of the often elusive nature of the choreographer/dancer's work, much less the pedagogy for transmitting this knowledge to undergraduate- and graduate-level students.

There are no specific or categorical "rules" for how a dance is made nor do universal rules for the making of a dancer exist. The processes are often deeply personal or intuitive. Because of their nonscientific nature, they resist objective taxonomy (Minton 1997). Therefore, this researcher's task was to look beyond these realities as limitations and to find equilibrium among theory, history, observation, deeply held beliefs, experiential analysis, and measurable data (Gibbons 1991).

The study was limited to dance programs within the United States in order to make certain that the teaching, learning, or employment process being examined exists within an American context and construct. Nonetheless, the origins and nearly all cultural influences on dance in America derive from European and some non-Western sources. It is the synthesis of these styles and techniques that have become embodied in American dancer training as well as college-level programs. However, to attempt to develop themes that would have application to programs outside the United States would not be consistent with what we know about the differing values that other countries place on identifying talent as well as their methods of developing such talent (Bloom 1985).

Snapshots and profiles of the identified institutions emerged through a retrospective-interview approach conducted with faculty and administrators of dance programs. The participants in each group consisted of those responding positively to requests to be included in the study. Potential respondents who could not be contacted by phone, mail, or e-mail were excluded from the study. Reasons for declining participation were not sought from those who were not interested in taking part in the study.

Data was collected over a period of three months. This brief window of time was used to attempt to measure only the institutions related to the participants and their respective programs. This study did not attempt to provide a comprehensive overview of all dance programs in the United States. While this researcher heard individual accounts from participants who related their personal experiences, this information cannot be used to represent all institutions and all programs. A review of historical artifacts, gathered through university mission statements, catalogs, factual university Web site pages, and other informational sources, were included in the study in order to provide a framework, context, and layers of meaning but was not intended to suggest a comprehensive picture of dance education programs throughout history or in the United States today. The researcher could only present information specific to the research question and the topics and subtopics within this investigation.

Reflectivity, in the form of analytic and personal memoing throughout data collection assisted in dissecting the research question and subtopics.

> Analytic memos not only capture analytic thinking about data, they facilitate such thinking, stimulating analytic insights. Memoing refers to any writing that the researcher does in relationship to the research (other than actual field notes, transcriptions or coding) and are an essential technique for qualitative analysis (Miles and Huberman 1994, 72).

Another researcher may find themes that are not the same as those found in these explorations, but evidence was provided through the recognition of ancillary topics and themes and as these emerged through the data. This information was acknowledged through the process of coding and analysis.

> Coding is the process whereby the researcher develops the concepts into categories and organizes the categories. The researcher looks to see what kinds of things were mentioned by participants many times (what themes appeared across the interviews). The researcher looks for possible relationships among the categories in the data (Johnson and Christensen, 2000, 336).

Results are not generalizable to the population or universe. The intention was to gain a clearer picture of the selected dance programs in this study.

Summary

The task of the choreographer or dancer has always been to discover and create a language and physical vocabulary ranging from an isolated simple gesture to movements of astonishing complexity. Whether attempting to heighten meaning within the ordinary, or creating sublime personal expression out of an interior emotional or spiritual impulse, the transcendent language of dance serves the universal need for individual expression as well as the yearning for that expression to be transferred through intentional connection to other human beings (Wagner 1997).

The ability of university-level dance education programs to prepare graduates for professional career paths is of primary significance to parents and students who are considering a decision that may ultimately require a sizeable investment of financial and other resources. As well, the merits of competing programs necessitate that each school substantiate with integrity its own claim for successfully providing sufficient—if not exemplary—career readiness. Finally, funding for a program obtained from within the institution as well as from outside revenue sources is often dependent upon demonstrating high standards as well as a history of outstanding accomplishments. This study endeavors to identify, to articulate, and to analyze the most effective principles and practices for sufficient preparation and readiness for careers in dance.

Chapter Two

Context of the Study

Introduction

This chapter will discuss the social and cultural aspects of dance and its influence on society. Areas of review in this chapter include dance and religion, secular dance, evolution of dance styles, classical dance, and the emergence of dance education. The historical review of dance and postsecondary dance education in this section is intended to provide a basic understanding of the nature of dance education in today's academy within the framework of its cultural importance.

Cultural, Social, and Religious Relevance of Dance

Dance, Anthropology, and Religion

Any examination of the role that an art form plays in human civilization involves studying the ways that particular discipline functions to reflect, comment upon, or provide future vision for the society that it inhabits. In terms of function, through dance the physical, emotional, intellectual, and spiritual powers of the body combine to communicate in a constant, fearless search to ask questions, challenge answers, and express meaning (Land 2000).

Dance can be defined as any type of human movement—from simple hand gestures by a single individual to complex ballets requiring many performers (Minton 2003). A finished choreographic work is also frequently enhanced with additional artistic elements, including music, text, costumes, scenery, lighting, and projections. Or dance can be deeply personal and may only involve a single expressive participant moving alone in the quiet of a room or in the expanse of outdoors. Laban (1948) envisioned a kind of populist dance for the masses. In *Body, Space, Expression: The Development of Rudolf Laban's Movement and Dance Concepts*, Vera Maletic (1987) describes the breadth of his conceptualization:

> Laban conceived of movement choirs as a medium providing experience of togetherness, as community through dance: "Thousands of people can now experience the benefit of the rhythm and flow of dance, not only as spectators but also as an active players [sic] in the joy of moving." However, he emphasized that besides the shared experience of the joyful movement, the crucial task of the movement choirs was to maintain a sense of humanity in a dignified form. He saw choral movement not as one of the many ways to achieve body-mind education but as the only possible way—for adults and children alike (1987, 14–15).

When dance is intentionally performed for an audience, a specific conscious agreement occurs: the observers experience the art while simultaneously engaged in a task virtually opposite that of the dancer's— *not moving* (Minton 2003).

As a significant means of communication in most societies throughout history, dance can be found as an integral component in tribal ritual and religious worship. Religion serves, especially in the absence of other social orders, to convey a society's values, understanding of its origins, purpose, and the ultimate destiny of humans. Wosien (1974) states, "Rituals of dance were man's intuitive way of attuning himself to the powers of the cosmos" (p. 19). Dreamlike forms were created and reiterated through rhythmic movement, providing the entry points to the inner source of life (Wosien, 1974).

Many religions use ritualistic gestures, evident in ceremonies, prayers, offerings, and adorations (Keali'inohomoku 1992). Because symbolism is a key element in dance, it was a particularly suitable medium, especially in more primitive or geographically remote regions, for evocation, provocation, persuasion, and reverence (Murphy 1986). Instances of dance employed in primitive worship have been discovered in the Efik culture of Nigeria to implore the gods for safe journey and fertility in childbirth and crops (de Mille 1961). Among the Ubacala, dancers are considered to be the reincarnation of ancestors, thereby linking the past and present;

dances are performed to induce trances among the members of the Kalahari; through dance healing powers endow the medicine men of the Kung of Namibia. Dance rituals routinely precede Amazonian hunting expeditions. Zulu war dances reenact and reinforce the strategies and tactics to be employed in addition to displaying the complimentary qualities of power, virility, and sexual display (Land 2000).

In early Greece, dance and choral song were the devotional focus of Terpsichore, the muse of dance and choral music and one of the nine Greek muses who were the daughters of Zeus and Mnemosyne. The Greeks considered dance to even have ethical qualities. As a means of discovering and becoming "who we are," they believe that dance communicates "the human condition in all of its ambiguity and paradox from despair and ecstatic joy to simply giving praise for life" (Brockett 2003, 24).

Dance, in varying degrees, is an important aspect in formalized Eastern religions. Hindu and Yoruba religions from two thousand years ago combined ceremonies, prayers, offerings, adorations, ritualistic gestures, storytelling, drumming, and dancing in order to achieve contact with gods and ancestors (Keali'inohomoku 1992). Two dance forms exemplify the way that religion, dance, and theater are synthesized in Indian life. The Indian dance forms are Bharatanatyam and Ottanthullal. The origins of Bharatanatyam can be traced to devotional dances performed in a Hindu temple. These are highly codified dances traditionally performed by a single female dancer (Ellfeldt 1976). By contrast, the Ottanthullal originated in the ancient storytelling tradition when Sanskrit epics were presented as temple offerings. Ottanthullal literally means "running and jumping." The solo artist dances, sings, and enacts an entire play without the use of a formal stage space and without the use of props (Shawn 1980). Like the Hindi religion, the Yoruba religion is steeped in tradition that includes dance as a ceremonial ritual. Yoruba worshippers communicate with gods and ancestors through dance and drumming. Some ceremonies are designed to induce possession, with the body of the worshipper providing the vehicle through which a god can visit earth (Land 2000).

* * * * *

Although the word *dance* occurs thirty-two times in the Old Testament and six times in the New Testament (Wagner, 401–406), dance in worship virtually disappeared during the early development of new Christian ceremonies and rites. However, as the Gospel proliferated beyond the geographic boundaries of the Greco-Roman regions, local dance traditions reappeared and again became incorporated into religious ceremonies (Shawn 1980). Within the solemn liturgical forms of the evolving rites in the Roman Catholic Church, ritual movements became stylized and formalized. Such strictly regulated liturgical practices mirrored the ideological and political control by the Papacy over both the organized body of Christ and the societies into which the church integrated itself during the years preceding the Protestant reformation (Kraus 1969). Specifically, controlled movements, such as the sign of the cross, were employed at specific points in prayer and communion during the holy sacrifice of the Mass. The priest, altar boys, and choirs processed, knelt, and chanted responsively in unison and at specifically selected moments and cues in the text or canonical action. There also existed a strong relationship between the reverent formality of movement and the architecture of the churches, particularly the sanctuaries. The skeletal "choreography" enacted in the sacramental spaces served to engender cohesiveness among all of the participants of the church service—singing with one voice, moving with one body (Wagner 1997).

For the next four centuries, in yet another reversal of thinking, any hint of dance in American Christianity—beyond the joining of hands in prayer—came to be considered immoral by "white, male, Protestant clergy and evangelists who argued from a narrow and selective interpretation of biblical passages" (Wagner 1997, 87). The core of the historic polemic against dance in America applied equally to participant and viewer. The debate grew to include issues of morals, manners, gender, social class, and race.

In spite of the continuous fluctuation between acceptance and banishment, dance in the Christian and Roman Catholic liturgies today has not been eliminated entirely, but incorporation requires a balance of sensibilities and sensitivities (de Mille 1961). In the past ten years, there has also been an increase in the number of choreographers interested in making sacred dance, often within the context of worship services (Hodes 1998). Indicative of the evolution of thinking, some Christian colleges are also now beginning to offer dance degrees (Fischer 1988).

Secular Dance

It is within the secular realm, outside the proscribed boundaries of the church's authority, that dance has maintained its strongest presence. In both eastern and western aristocracies, court dance represented the power and hierarchical privilege of the ruling monarchy. Connotations and references to status, wealth, and military prowess existed within the dances themselves, most evident and openly demonstrated via intricate systems of partnering and floor placement. Social etiquette as well as aesthetic refinement gained expression through both the dance steps as well as the codification of these movements into European dance manuals. Through commissioning ballets and subsidizing tours, a system of patronage and employment contributed to the goal for enhancement and preservation of the culture. Extensions of the above practices manifest themselves today throughout the world in national outpourings and displays of respect or solidarity embodied in coronations, weddings, funerals, and commemorative ceremonies (Land 2002).

Through the centuries, dance has played a vital role among the ruling aristocracy of many societies. In fact, it was often considered to be the duty of the monarch to dance well in order to honor the source of his power and to reinforce the court hierarchy. While this characteristic was humorously exemplified by Yul Brynner in the stage and film performances of *The King and I*, the power and privilege of the monarchy indeed gave court dances unique characteristics that are still recognizable today in traditional court dances (Flinn 1997). The principle purposes of court dance are the following:

1. To display power, such as wealth and military prowess.
2. To confer privilege or status on the participants, as in exclusive balls. In traditional court dances, one's status was shown by when, where, and with whom one danced.
3. To exemplify refinement through movement that is considered elegant, serene, beautiful, and noble. European dance manuals provided guidance for social etiquette as well as for dance steps.
4. To preserve culture, such as in the Japanese Imperial Court's preservation of Bugaku—the world's oldest recorded, continuously performed dance.
5. To enhance culture through patronage such as court-commissioned ballets and state department tours (Brown 1979).

Variations of the court dance archetype live on in a modern society demonstrating that ceremonial displays continue to fulfill a purpose in a largely democratic world. This is evident today in occasions such as weddings, funerals, military functions, and other national ceremonies.

Dance at Social Gatherings

Social dancing appears in almost every free society in some form or another, revealing cultural attitudes toward sex, gender, race, and socio-economic status as well as playing an important role in identity development. Young men and women learn about the behavior expected of them and begin to exercise the gender roles society has assigned them. In the Polynesian Islands, students spend two hours of their school day receiving instruction from a dance master in the traditional dances of their culture (Martin 1952). The importance of cultural preservation is also transmitted through rituals and dances passed from one generation to the next, underscoring the message of familial and tribal affiliation (Land 2000).

Since ancient times, public rites of passage are also important contexts for dances within a societal construct (Murphy 1986, 98). The specific meanings of such dances mark and celebrate transition, whether it be death rites among the Merina of Madagascar or the boys' initiations in southeast Angola. This same functional power manifests itself in American traditions such as homecoming, cotillions, and the first dance at a wedding reception accorded specifically to the bride and her father (Murphy 1986).

In some societies, social dancing is segregated; men and women do not dance with each other at all and, in fact, are not permitted to dance in the same locations. In other societies, men and women dance as couples but never touch. Historically, social dances once were considered to be scandalous (Wright 2003). An example of this is found in the waltz introduced in the early 1900s. This new dance shocked the refined upper class because it was so different from the minuet. In the waltz, couples held hands and danced side by side. The waltz contrasted with the stylized minuet that was more formal and far less intimate and so a minimum of touching occurred (Grody 1998).

An outgrowth of the minuet and waltz is the popular and highly social form known as ballroom dancing. International in scope and popularity, ballroom dancing was originally the domain of polite society in the royal court. Today, dances such as the fox-trot, swing, polka, cha-cha, and many more are performed to popular music and cuts across many social classes and ethnic boundaries (McDonagh 1986).

The American public's consciousness of human movement as an integral component of everyday life has expanded dramatically since 1980 with the proliferation of dance in film, television, MTV, and the aerobic fitness movement. The paradigm has expanded from a strict view as merely art. Dance and movement are now readily associated with health, lifestyle, nutrition, and self-image (Wilson 1986).

In the 1990s, dance became a dominant element in mass media, advertising, and interactive technology. In the most "hip" contemporary social context, secular dance today is manifested in the contemporary club scene of Generation X. Here a synthesis of techno music, lights, and drugs combine to create an entire experience of multisensory bombardment for crowds of several hundreds. Finally, secular dance even exists within a controversial context when definitions of free speech and public taste clash in communities in which there are concerted and often divisive efforts to foster standards of decency by creating and enforcing local ordinances governing dance as adult entertainment (Fischer 1988).

The Impact of Human Migration and Cultural Mixing on Dance Forms

In the early 1700s, a massive human migration brought Europeans to North and South America in search of religious freedom and a solution to improving their social and economic condition (Long 1995). Africans, on the other hand, did not travel to either continents of the New World of their own accord, and then were subjugated to slavery on Confederate plantations. For slaves taken from their birth societies, dance helped to preserve an important part of their heritage (Land 2000).

In South America, the European settlers were lenient and allowed African slaves to retain their dances and drumming and to fuse their religious beliefs with those of Christianity. In North America, however, the European influence produced a different fusion of African and European dance forms. Africans were not allowed to dance for their own gods. Plantation owners feared that the rituals would lead to a slave rebellion. Dancing was permitted for entertainment only, so the slaves began gradually to imitate their masters, satirically disguising their mocking by blending elements of rhythm and improvisation with movement (Long 1995).

Eventually, dances created by African Americans became very popular in white society, such as in the 1930s when the Lindy Hop caused a national sensation (Wright 2003). The Charleston, jitterbug, and even disco derive elements from the vocabulary that had been retained and then cross-fertilized with American culture. Jazz dance today is inseparably linked to African dance (Kraines 2001).

In the 1970s, a striking example of fusion between the European and African cultures is to be found in American street dancing (Kerr 1992). Here, Irish jig and English clog merged with "buck dancing" (a product of black plantation culture) when Africans traveled to northern industrial cities seeking better job opportunities (Long 1995). Inner city street corners become the petri dishes for nurturing a cultural revolution based in movement and provided a vehicle for the unheard voices of marginalized and economically disadvantaged populations (Kerr 1992).

Although the ascension of rap in the 1990s is considered to be a stunning cultural phenomenon, its Afrocentric antecedents are readily apparent:

> Because of the interrelationship between African dance and vocal/rhythmic music, it is particularly worth noting the similar interchange that occurs between rap vocalists and their dancers. This interrelationship is apparent in the dancers who often accompany many rappers. As popular forms, these dances are not only partially African-derived but also draw from a host of other dance forms. Consequently, they are constantly redefining and reinterpreting themselves to produce new forms (Kerr 1992, 56).

The sociological implications of these connections are evident, but the recent emergence to eminence of the rapper Eminem, a Caucasian artist, represents an unparalleled shift in sensibility as well as in the power of marketing and telecommunications to synthesize historically polarized cultural attitudes and their artistic manifestations and representations (Bozza 2002). Clearly, Afrocentric forms have played a major role in the evolution of American dance.

During the thirties and forties, motion pictures became accessible to the public, and large numbers of Americans flocked to films featuring the elegant dancing of Fred Astaire and Ginger Rogers or the kaleidoscopic choreography of Busby Berkeley. The big band era of Duke

Ellington, Benny Goodman, Count Basie, Artie Shaw, and the Dorsey brothers brought dance music to the masses aided by the technological revolution that made possible widespread use of the radio and phonograph records (McDonagh 1986). By the 1950s, freedom in dance had come to a new generation of teenagers epitomized in the national adolescent embracing of Elvis Presley. The social order of subsequent decades is largely an outgrowth of the response by that first generation that was introduced to rock and roll (Ellfeldt 1976).

Two Classical Dance Forms—Ballet and Kabuki

Ballet and Kabuki are classical dance theater forms that remain popular today although they were both created more than three hundred years ago (Lee 1987). Similar in nature, although very different in outward expression, both express the beliefs and values of their founding cultures via highly theatrical staging of dramatic and romantic stories. Both forms flourished in the 1800s and 1900s and survived through patron support. Ballet and Kabuki represent major distinctions between Eastern and Western cultures, as well as important bridges between the past and the present (de Mille 1961).

Ballet was an outgrowth of early European court dances. The first actual ballet dates to 1581 when the Ballet Comique de la Reine performed at the court of Henry III of France at Fontainebleau (de Mille 1961). The ballet was produced by the queen mother, Catherine de Medici, and was developed throughout the centuries to mean a theatrical storytelling through dance (Garfunkel 1994). The Encyclopedia of Diderot (1772) states, "Ballet is action explained by a dance . . . specifically theatrical, spectacular, and done to be seen. . . ."

Beginning in the twentieth century, the dancer's skirts got shorter and soft slippers—the forerunners of the ballet shoe as we know it—were adopted. As the practical authority of the monarchies declined, the wealthy upper classes assumed the leadership necessary to financially sustain all of the arts. Patronage of the ballet included the benefits of influence, visibility, and authority. Ballet's continuing appeal into this century has endured through the classicism of its music and movement vocabulary, but also not insignificantly from the philanthropic support of affluent benefactors and audiences (Anderson 1977).

Formalization of instruction in ballet flourished as a result of the cultural explosion taking place. It was in the French courts during the

reign of Louis XIV that a standardized methodology was not only codified but also recorded in great detail. *Orchesography*, a 1589 book by
Thoinot Arbeau set out a series of basic principles and vocabulary that
continues to be the basis for ballet instruction throughout the world (1589).

Unlike ballet, Kabuki originated as street entertainment for the lower
classes in Japan. Created in 1600 by Okuni, Kabuki was comprised of
large ensemble dances performed by women. Kabuki is generally passed
down through generations within a family of Kabuki players, and most
work for years on developing and maturing a single role. The greatest
Kabuki players may continue to perform throughout their seventies (Land
2002).

Dance in the Twentieth Century

The evolutionary thought and practices within the arts and humanities
often mirror the rapid changes and advances throughout societies in industry, trade, medicine, the environment, religious-political thinking,
and communications. Just as America, in the early 1900s, was transformed by the inventions of the automobile, the electric lightbulb, the
telephone, and the radio, so also American choreographers and their
disciples revolutionized the art of dance (Anderson 1977).

Isadora Duncan (1877–1927), known as the mother of modern dance,
revolutionized the art form by rejecting standard ballet forms and send-
ing her own personal dance vision into the world (Hall 1972). Duncan
threw away the corsets, ballet slippers, pointed shoes, and tutus. She
danced barelegged and barefoot in a short Greek tunic (Erkert 2003).
Her performances were not theatrical in a traditional or accepted context. Her choreography was not based in the telling of stories or exhibi-
tion of brilliant technique as were characteristic of classical ballet. Hers
was an art of personal expression. Duncan's movements were simple—
running and skipping accompanied by moderate lifts and leaps (Mazo
1977).

Following Duncan's lead, standard ballet forms were rejected by
other dancers. Storytelling was eliminated as the basis of choreography
in favor of emotional expression and purer explorations of composition.
There was no emphasis on brilliant technique. Dancers performed barefoot. The modern dancer's instinct to be grounded in the earth replaced
the ballet dancer's aspiration to defy gravity. Maud Allen's (1873–1952)
style of interpretive dancing also helped expand the definitions of mod-

ern dance. At the height of her success, she was as well known as Isadora Duncan (Grein 1908). She danced to critical acclaim and toured the world. Ruth St. Denis and Ted Shawn of the Denishawn School (1914–1940) continued to stretch the boundaries of the dance paradigm (Mazo 1977). Their movement vocabularies were highly individualistic. The aesthetic emphasis on displaying the musculature of the body as presented through turned-out positions was replaced by a vocabulary emphasizing flexed feet and turned-in or parallel positions initiated by contractions from the center of the body (Penrod 1998).

In the late 1940s and early 1950s, a new group of individualistic, creative choreographers again revolutionized dance performance in America. They maintained the effort to free the art form of dance from the conventions and restraints of their predecessors. Dancer-choreographer Martha Graham, who offered her first dance concert in New York City in 1926, grew into this new socially conscious dance generation and firmly established the new concept that the choreographer as well as the dancer could use movement for personal expression instead of storytelling. She has generally been accepted as the greatest single figure in American modern dance (Doeser 1980).

Doris Humphrey's work was compared to Graham's in that it was modern, but she was more concerned with gravity and an evocation of mood than Graham's sense of drama (Erkert 2003). Hanya Holm, while not an outstanding dancer herself, was a wonderful teacher and influenced the teachings of many dance educators (Kraus 1969). George Balanchine, director of the New York City Ballet, brought American qualities to traditional ballet vocabulary and form by incorporating uniquely American-flavored musical elements of syncopation, speed, and energy (Buckle 1988) exemplified in works such as *The Four Temperaments* and *Symphony in C* (Martin 1952). Katherine Dunham, a dancer-anthropologist, found inspiration and identity in her African American heritage using her roots to introduce the unusual and physically challenging idea of body isolations, especially when done simultaneously to different rhythms (Beckford 1979). It is important to note the prevailing Afrocentric influence on American modern dance beyond Dunham's contribution.

With a direct departure from the criteria that had previously defined the European classical dance vocabulary, the development of American modern dance represented a new way of perceiving the body as a medium of artistic expression. Subsequently, this affected the body's

potential for movement. The result was the invention of a new movement vocabulary that included baring the feet, allowing the spine to
curve and become more supple, and working closer to the ground. All
these characteristics can be linked to similar elements in African dance
. . . (1) how energy is utilized in the body, (2) use of weight, and (3)
improvisation (Kerr 1992, 56, 58).

In 1943, American musical theater as we know it today was revolutionized by Agnes de Mille's choreography for *Oklahoma*. For the first
time, dances were consciously devised and integrated into the plot with
the specific intention of furthering the forward dramatic momentum of
the storyline (1961). Such function was exemplified by Jerome Robbins
with his 1957 choreography for *West Side Story* (as well as his adaptation
of the dances for the camera in the 1961 film version of this musical)
(Garfunkel 1994). Other choreographers who have broken the mold for
the American musical stage include Jack Cole, Grover Dale, Joe Layton,
Gower Champion, Graciela Danielle, Patricia Birch, Gwen Verdon, Ann
Reinking, Michael Bennett, Bob Fosse, Tommy Tune, and Susan
Strohman (Flinn 1997).

Historically, dance artists have depended on well-intentioned benefactors to financially support their choreographic endeavors. During the
favorable funding climate of the sixties and seventies, a proliferation of
new dance companies pushed the envelope of choreographic and performance possibilities in America. Led by such visionaries as Merce
Cunningham, Doug Varone, Louis Falco, Paul Taylor, Trisha Brown,
Molissa Fenley, Bella Lewitsky, Erik Hawkins, Twyla Tharp, Steve
Paxton, Lar Lubovitch, Mark Morris, Bill T. Jones/Arnie Zane, Alvin
Ailey, Garth Fagan and ensembles such as the Alwin Nikolais Dance
Theatre and Pilobolus, choreographers today have not only continued to
invent and redefine techniques built upon the old but have also proposed
new, daring personal visions of what dancing can be (Hodes 1998). Indeed, if one characteristic applies to all contemporary dance makers, it is
the insistence on moving in response to their own inner voices and emotional rhythms, inventing in the best work a new vocabulary of movement, gesture, and personal belief that speaks an ever-evolving yet universal language of dance (Dupont 1977).

The Explosion of the American Commercial Dance Industry

The performance industry for dancers offers employment in the non-profit as well as commercial sectors. New York and Los Angeles are generally considered the meccas of the commercial sector. While many would argue that the heartbeat of the nonprofit world is also to be found in New York, one only needs to review professional directories to discover thriving environments for ballet and modern dance companies in all the major metropolitan areas of the United States. Regional companies provide outstanding entry-level opportunities for young performers. Many regional opera companies hire dancers on per production basis. Musicals such as *42nd Street, Wonderful Town*, and *Dames at Sea* entertainingly tell the classic stories of young talent coming to New York City with the hopes of "getting that big break" and performing on Broadway or with the Rockettes (Mirault 1998). Performers in such Broadway productions today typically must be able to dance, sing, act, and provide a characterization onstage inhabiting an entire emotional understanding of the play as well as embodying the particular production style. If such a young performer possesses these multiple skills, he/she has the potential to audition and be hired for a wide variety of other commercial work outside the very small circle of opportunities on Broadway or national touring companies, including regional theater and dinner theater, the cruise line industry, trade and industrial shows, Las Vegas entertainment, and the music video industry. Dancing for a living in the commercial sector requires that the aspiring young performer have both the technical, emotional, and economic tools to be constantly looking for "the next job." It is a highly competitive industry governed by people whose focus is to generate profits as a return on substantial investments (Paul 2003).

This extended dance landscape also includes performing opportunities in an enormous entertainment business that provides highly produced dance revue shows outside of the United States utilizing almost exclusively the talents of American dancers. Hundreds of American dancers are employed each year in productions in Guam, Japan, Mexico City, and Acapulco. Contract ranges typically are a minimum of nine months with options for renewal. Dancers frequently are able to save their earnings and meet their day-to-day living expenses from per diem compensation. Work in these productions is jazz- and theater-dance oriented, but solid ballet technique is the foundation for such styles and so the caliber of talent auditioning for work of this kind is exceptionally high (Mirault 1994).

A thriving cruise line industry is thriving and provides steady employment to dancers who meet the rigorous technical criteria necessary to perform in this highly competitive arm of the entertainment business. A dancer usually performs in four or five different shows whose themes usually showcase particular composers or dance styles. The major employers are the Disney Cruise Lines, Carnival Cruise Lines, Royal Caribbean Cruise Lines, and Norwegian Cruise Lines (Paul 2003).

Las Vegas still markets itself as the entertainment capital of the world and provides steady work for dancers. Contracts consist of constantly rotated and updated fifteen shows of as short a length as fifteen minutes. Advantages to employment in this resort industry are longevity of contract plus benefits because the dancers actually are contracted employees of the various hotels. Smaller markets for this same kind of work opportunity in entertainment can be found in Orlando (Florida), Nashville (Tennessee), and Branson (Missouri) (Mirault 1998).

Young dancers may also find employment with production companies that subcontract to develop and produce entire entertainment packages, spectacular events, or theatrical presentations worldwide. Theme parks such as Six Flags, with locations in major cities like Atlanta, Dallas, and San Jose, utilize the services of production companies. Once hired in one city, dancers have the advantage of being able to work consistently in any of these multiple locations. Other major theme parks that utilize hundreds of dancers are Disney, Universal Studios, Nickelodeon, and Opryland. Two categories of dance work offered by these theme parks are (1) "parade dancers" who are performers and characters hired for specialty parades and (2) special production dancers hired for limited-run shows such as "animazement" that are based on topical themes or current media trends and then put to rest as new special productions are conceived and created (Boling 2000).

Trade and industrial shows are live entertainments in which entertainment used to promote a new product or line of products (ranging from cars to power equipment to computers) or to train workers with new information in an industry field. Such productions typically involved a large scope and budget in order to create maximum impact. Industrial shows are often only performed one time and are financially very lucrative to dancers. Once one breaks successfully into the pool of reliable and available talent for these demanding contracts, a dancer can work very steadily. Other advantages are short-term contracts with high compensation, variety of choreographic styles, and travel (Paul 2003).

Finally, work in the MTV/music video industry provides extensive work to dancers, although there exists considerable confusion within the industry as to the merits of employment due to the many unanswered questions relating to equitable compensation pertaining to technology issues and the dissemination of images via computer, Internet, DVD, MP3s, and the iPod. Until litigation provides industrywide standards, work in this field is not considered to be entirely protected (Mirault 1994).

Dancing in One World

Telecommunications and travel options transforming the world into a global village have had a profound influence on the field of dance in America. At the beginning of the twenty-first century, dance is still expressing society's values; it is a means for people to achieve a sense of harmony, identity, and balance within an ever-changing and complex world. Dance continues to assist many societies in maintaining and sustaining their heritages, functioning in the major role of culture recorder (Land 2000).

Dance also continues to reflect political and social concerns. Considerable work has been made to demystify this art form and diminish its elitist image. The pioneering work of Liz Lerman has bridged the isolation between artists and the elderly and set the stage for the work of other dancers to work with underserved or marginalized populations (Cleveland 1992). The belief that anyone can dance regardless of ability or disability is further reinforced by the work of companies such as Dancing Wheels in Cleveland and the New Visions program of Very Special Arts that provide opportunities for populations often self-stigmatized and who traditionally do not seek access to the arts. Through dance, individuals and groups explore what it means to be who they are, what makes them unique, and what they have in common living in a world in which geographic location no longer limits access to participation (Cleveland 1992).

Dance in Education

Claims of the Arts, Dance, and Education

Educational authority C. Robert Pace (1969) spoke out in recognition of the contribution of the arts to total education. He suggested there was a need for another kind of learning in both childhood and higher education:

> The language of movement and form, of color, and of sequence, and sound, the languages of direct expression and feeling. Throughout history, these have been powerful and significant avenues by which man has expressed his knowledge, his aspirations, his beliefs, his insights and his wisdom. Are these still foreign languages to many of our students? Is the capacity to translate them, to understand their meaning, and to communicate through them teachable? If we must require competence in two languages for graduation from college, why not the languages of painting and sculpture, of drama and dance or of music? (Pace 1969, 268).

Pace's clarity of thought foreshadowed what today has become an entire educational movement calling for the arts to be included and ensured as basic in K–12 education. Acclaimed dancer, choreographer, and National Institute of Dance founder Jacques D'Amboise (1934–) explains his justification for the teaching of dance in public schools:

> In order to be free, in order to create, in order to learn, a student has to have limits imposed by his teacher. Students have to be given a framework within which to create. If you tell a class to "make up anything you like," what you get is chaos. But impose a limit, "Make up anything you like, but do it in one-foot square," and you have the beginnings of creative thinking. Add another limit: "Now still in one-foot square, invent some movements that last thirty seconds (not twenty-five or thirty-two, it has to be thirty), and you've introduced the concept of time . . . This exercise, this imposition of limits, defines choreography. Choreography is the communication of an idea, using ordered and structured gesture, in time (a thirty-second rag) and space (one-foot square). A far cry from chaos (D'Amboise, Cooke, and George 1983, 32).

Bolstered by the pleasure of hard-earned autonomy coming to fruition within postsecondary institutions, dance educators needed to then begin directing their energies toward more precisely articulating their own essential values and purposes. Six main areas of purpose for dance in education of all ages were identified:

1. Movement Education. An important thrust of physical education with a particular appeal with the enjoyment that it gives the participant; important values for people of all ages but has been seen as a vital element in the overall personality development of a child.
2. Development of Personal Creativity. Enhances and encourages the personal creativity of students; through compositional problems, the student is encouraged to develop imaginative and inventive thinking and solutions.
3. Aesthetic Experience. An aesthetic opportunity is provided to students through dance; they are aware of the aesthetic experience and are able to respond to artistic stimuli and increasingly able to express themselves through a creative outlet.
4. Intercultural and Integrative Experience. Dance provides a medium for understanding the customs, attitudes, and history of people of other cultures. Through the study of folk and ethnic dance, students may get a firsthand knowledge of an intercultural experience that leads to a fuller sense of unity, harmony, and awareness of other lands and their people.
5. Social Involvement. Provides an opportunity for group involvement and encourages intense, positive social interaction and interpersonal relationships in small groups.
6. Carryover Values. Dance can be viewed as preparation for future leisure activities and may be enjoyed as an activity throughout a person's life (Kraus and Chapman 1991).

In a policy statement from the National Dance Association Project on *Issues and Concerns in Dance Education* sponsored by the Alliance for Arts Education (with funding from the Office of Education of the U.S. Department of Health, Education and Welfare), the following justifications for dance within the curriculum were cited:

1. Dance is basic education, intensifying and clarifying the human experience.

2. Dance reinforces all learning, relating to and enhancing other academic areas.
3. Dance provides an alternative to the usual modes of education and is valuable in reaching students who may not respond to the more formal modes of teaching.
4. Dance promotes self and social awareness, helping students confront and understand themselves and cooperate effectively with others.
5. Dance promotes good health and may be of particular value of students with physical or mental disabilities.
6. Dance promotes fuller understanding of one's own culture and that of other peoples (Fowler and Little 1977, 10–13).

Regardless of whether a student is exposed to dance in any K–12 setting in states having curriculum guidelines or mandates, after-school and weekend classes are available—even in rural settings—at local private studios. It is interesting to note that no state requires a dance credential for dance educators teaching in these studios (Hanna 1999).

Evolution of Dance Programs in American Postsecondary Education

Justification for the value of dance at the postsecondary level requires a comprehension and unwavering defense of this intrinsic, holistic, essential benefit and its effectiveness when applied as a valid component of higher education.

> The study of dance can have tremendous impact on the college student by helping to facilitate problem finding and problem solving. It also fosters recognition of learning processes, working processes, and studying processes, as well as awareness of how one functions within a group and within interpersonal relationships. The characteristics establish dance as a rejuvenator and builder of the individual, who is then better able to approach the rest of the curriculum with the same sense of connection, vision, and creative insight (Abrams 1991, 10).

The emergence of dance performance and instruction at the college and university level in America begins in 1913 and is represented by the journey from an insignificant frill in physical education departments to large-budget, viable, sustainable, and thriving undergraduate and graduate degree programs on over three hundred campuses nationwide.

In the early part of the century, the most popular forms of dance taught in postsecondary institutions were tap and clog, folk and national dance. Three pioneering women rather bravely departed from such traditional curriculum and built the basis or foundation for dance education in America, as we know it today. Turn-of-the-century fundamentalism provided a backdrop of moral fervor that passionately resisted each encroachment of a society undergoing profound social change. Thus, the work of Gertrude Colby, Bird Larson, and Margaret H'Doubler was "groundbreaking and consistent with the sweeping changes in American society exemplified by black migration to the North, waves of European immigration, expanding public schools, and women in the workforce" (Wagner 1997, 236).

Colby developed a movement-training program for children K–12 termed "natural dance" at Columbia City Teachers College. This program was developed between 1913 and 1916. She incorporated the educational views of John Dewey (1859–1952) that encouraged the uniqueness of each child. She was experimenting with rhythmic, natural, and expressive movement yet was able to provide a new approach to dance programs that could still exist within a traditional educational framework (Kraus and Chapman, 1981).

In 1914, Larson, a former student of Colby's, also became a leading figure in the development of dance education. She initiated the first dance courses at Barnard College and used Colby's curriculum program from Columbia as a model. These courses added a strong emphasis on technique while for the first time also combining a foundation of information pertaining to anatomy, kinesiology, and physiology. Larson went beyond movement to emphasize technical control. Larson's program began to move dance education toward a more codified and scientific study of the human body as related to the biomechanics of movement (Kraus and Chapman 1981).

Creative dance—a term used to emphasize free and unstructured movement, self-discovery and spontaneous response to music—was introduced by H'Doubler (herself a basketball coach and a student of Colby and Larson's), who in 1919 offered the University of Wisconsin's first dance course. In 1926, creative dance matured to become the nation's first dance degree program established at the college level. During her forty years as an educator, H'Doubler taught hundreds of teachers, clarified the educational principles underlying dance in education, and organized Orchesis, a college dance club that had many chapters in the United States. These chapters continued to proliferate during the forty years of her teaching (Kraus and Chapman 1981).

It is also noteworthy that the foreword to H'Doubler's book *The Dance and Its Place in Education* (1927) is written by F. Louise Nardin, who was then dean at the University of Wisconsin at Madison. Her rationale for dance on her campus and in higher education is framed exclusively by her belief in the advantages of women's education (Ferdun 1990). Over sixty years later, Van Dyke (1992) offered this proposal:

> Providing a context for what is being taught will give students a clearer picture of a world in which they can make choices, as will linking a particular technique to a belief system . . . We do want to give students the skills required for moving with power and articulation. That sense of control is, I think, what draws many young women to the field, giving them a realm where they feel certain empowerment (1992, 31).

Often neglected in the general overview of dance at the postsecondary level is the role played by several pioneering, persevering spirits at Oberlin College in Oberlin, Ohio. Contrary to prevailing policy in the late nineteenth century, Oberlin did not ban dance as an extracurricular activity, but strongly promoted the sound integration of physical and mental activities. In 1885, Delphine Hanna, originally trained as a doctor at Harvard, became the first female professor of physical education in the United States. She included aesthetic dance in her curriculum, modeled on the Delsarte system of codified physical gestures that represent interior emotional states (Kirstein 1942). H'Doubler's work was incorporated into the curriculum during the 1920s. What had begun as an innovative work had now been sustained for over thirty years, just as many other colleges and universities were only beginning to explore the incorporation of dance into curriculum (Hanna 1999). Sally Houston continued to develop the program, and in 1964, Betty Lind shifted the focus from the primarily educational dance tradition to place the courses within the Oberlin theater program. Experimental work in the early 1970s included a residency by Steve Paxton that is generally acknowledged to have been the genesis of contact improvisation. A former Oberlin student named Brenda Way then replaced Lind. Her work led to the formation of the Oberlin Dance Collective, a company that eventually found a new artistic home in San Francisco in 1976. As a microcosm of dance in postsecondary settings, Oberlin's contribution cannot be disregarded and is consistent with the college's other visionary policies for women and blacks and many other areas of social and political reform (Woodward 1999).

By 1931, the American Association for Physical Education—AAPE (which later became the American Association for Health, Physical Education and Recreation - AAHPER) established a separate division for dance, encouraging leadership and becoming the leading force in promoting dance education throughout the United States through its workshops, publications, advisory services, and production of major dance events (Beiswanger 1960). Smith, Vassar, Wellesley, Barnard, New York University, and the University of Michigan all sponsored symposiums on dance education during the 1930s and eventually professional dance companies were also brought to these institutions of higher learning for performances and workshops (Hanna 1999).

In 1934, the Bennington School of Dance was instituted at Bennington College in Vermont; and professional modern dance artists such as Martha Graham, Hanya Holm, Doris Humphrey, Charles Weidman, and Louis Horst presented work to students between 1934 and 1942 (Brown 1979). In 1937, according to Eugene C. Howe, the extraordinary rise of modern dance was credited to be "the most recent event of major importance in physical education" (Howe 1937, 132). The Bennington program, by bringing together, for the first time dance educators in an intensive, rarified working atmosphere, forever raised the bar for achievement in both technical challenge and approaches to dance composition in postsecondary instruction (Mazo 1977). More importantly, it accomplished consciousness-raising for another key group of decision makers:

> The effect of this nudge from the professional world was to establish in the minds of university administrators the realization that dance was more than just an activity in physical education; it was a potentially legitimate art form worthy of taking a place among the other arts . . . dance educators [could eventually be] freed of the conceptual limitations that had been imposed upon them by the assumption that dance was merely a subdivision of physical education (Hayes 1977, 341).

The onset of World War II ended the swift rise of dance programs like those at Bennington College (Mazo 1977). Still, a steadfast vision of dance as a vital force in American education continued. In 1948, as the war was ending, Connecticut College began a summer school in dance where students were exposed to Hungarian-born intellectual Rudolf von Laban's (1971) theories of movement, philosophies, and teaching approach. His contribution of dance and human movement theory was another major influence on the emerging scene. His most important work was his analysis of the physical laws of movement as applied to dance training (Brown 1979).

By 1950, visitors and artists in residence at Connecticut College, including Jose Limon, Sophie Maslow, Pearl Primus, Merce Cunningham, Humphrey, and many more, brought different viewpoints and insight to the world of dance and dance teaching (Mazo 1977). By 1957, sixty works had been premiered and one hundred eighty-nine dances had been performed at Connecticut College. More than one hundred fifty summer students from thirty states and seven foreign countries attended the summer school that year. In 1969, the summer school had three hundred nineteen students and a full-time faculty of thirty-five. In 1978, the summer school moved to Duke University in Durham, North Carolina, and began to sponsor an annual critic's conference, an annual dance television workshop, dance therapy workshops, an annual dance educator's weekend, and an annual community outreach program (Lloyd 1972).

Results of a 1955 comprehensive survey (the first *College and University Dance Directory*) revealed the placement of dance programs in higher education (Ingram 1986, 194):

Departments	Percent
Physical Education	73%
Dance	11%
Theater	5%
Dance in Physical Education	5%
Dance in education	3%
Dance in fine arts	3%

By 1955, dance departments were actively seeking out programmatic solutions to the many philosophic questions being asked on individual campuses as well as in the national dialogues for physical education within academia. Within this context, it is useful to recognize several pertinent benchmarks in the twentieth century (Ingram 1986, 195):

Year	Benchmark
1905	American Association for Health, Physical Education, and Recreation (AAHPER) President Luther Gulick sets dance as theme of 1905 conference.
1931	Section status for dance is submitted to the AAPE and is granted by President Mabel Lee.
1932	The dance section is accepted by AAPE governing board.
1933	A high school study is established to develop dance curriculums for the high schools.
1956	Committee to study dance therapy is formed to examine the prerequisites for dance therapists.
1965	"Dance as a Discipline" is topic at Boulder, Colorado, conference.
1965	The National Endowment for the Arts (NEA) is created to encourage and assist the nation's cultural resources with the mission "to foster the excellence, diversity, and vitality of the arts in the United States."
1965	Arts and humanities governmental policies enable dance faculty to apply and receive federal funding to move out of physical education departments as dance is accorded status as an art form.
1970-71	U.S. Office of Education funds project IMPACT. Informal coalition results among directors of the Dance, Art, Music, and Theater (DAMT) associations.
1979	Dance achieves alliance status when the word "dance" is added to title of AAHPER making it AAHPERD

Throughout the rapid expansion immediately following World War II, dance educators began to try to identify their basic objectives and explain their theoretical rationale for dance in higher education. Because it was perceived as a skill or activity within physical education, it was expected to contribute to the following four philosophical educational goals: (1) organic development, (2) neuromuscular development, (3) interpretive development, and (4) personal-social development. However, none of these goals implied any great emphasis on creative or aesthetic expression or technical or artistic merit. Generally, dance was still not respected or treated as a valid art form within most postsecondary educational institutions (Ingram 1986).

Beginning in the 1960s, many students began to question and reject the academic values that they claimed were being imposed upon them. They rallied for flexibility in planning their curriculum course of study. They increasingly demanded greater relevance and sought more significant forms of personal expression and meaning in their education. An increasing number of students took courses concerned with humanistic lifestyles, ethnic history, women's issues, and similar contemporary interests. Academic standards relaxed. Alternative education, independent study, and open universities became popular (Kraus and Chapman 1981).

Also, during the 1960s, campus trends in social activism were reflecting the movements in America toward dismantling various forms of prejudice and discrimination. Juxtaposed to these shifting attitudes remained the reality that historical factors and harmful myths contribute to the social message that dance is not an acceptable activity for males (Poole 1986). This evolving consciousness presented a dilemma to institutions of higher education that had no guide or precedent for addressing the systemic roots of this problem. Ferdun (1990) asks whether

> race, social class, ethnic, political, and sexual orientations may be classifications that need special study not only to fill out the picture of who is being served in dance in higher education but also to ensure against the preclusion or promotion of particular groups or ideas simply by virtue of the unexamined traditions of the history of dance in higher education (1990, 8).

Two additional issues arose in the sixties. A major concern existed over which style of modern dance technique should be taught. Traditional factions favored Graham and Humphrey while others espoused Nikolais or Cunningham (Garfunkel 1994). Academic-degree requirements presented the second area of division (Hanna 1999). Debate centered on "legitimizing" professional dancers for teaching within higher education by finding a balance between their own creative efforts in performance or choreography against the expectation of contributing to the field through research and publications (Oliver 1992, 3).

By the seventies, the maturing of thought in postsecondary dance programs required an addressing of the distinction between "training" and "education" in order to move forward with the clarification of institutional standards. Answers to these questions would not only have an impact on funding justifications, but would be necessary in order to maintain integrity in marketing and recruitment efforts.

Technical training and philosophical premises of a liberal arts education have never fit comfortably together. Because university dance programs have traditionally required creative and/or scientific work and theoretical study, while sometimes downplaying the importance of technical training, they have tended to attract and develop dancers more interested in ideas and individual expression than those trained entirely in professional studios (Van Dyke 1992, 27).

The possibility that postsecondary dance programs might be providing a disservice to its students raised serious considerations for practitioners and leaders in sectors including nonprofit performing companies, for-profit entertainment industries, and philanthropy. Ingram argues that the core issue remains the same:

My perception is that, before 1970, university dance students normally went on to become the dancer/teachers or dancer/scholars of the field, with only a small percentage making a career of performing. This lack of emphasis on technique in the academic curriculum allowed universities and colleges to graduate students in four years, though many were, at that point, not employable as professional dancers. Thus, in spite of apparent common interests, a schism developed between the academic dance world and the professional field, reflecting a deep divergence of values centering on the question of whether one is trying to train the dancer or educate the person, to teach skills or build inner resources (Kraus and Chapman 1981, 158).

By 1981, the National Association of Schools of Dance (NASD) had been formed in recognition of the need to create accreditation standards for an association of educational programs in dance. Initially, forty-eight institutions became charter members, including thirty-eight colleges and universities. A polemic rift continued, however, as the incompatibility between athletic programs and dance was juxtaposed against an American culture increasingly obsessed with body image, sports, and entertainment.

In the mideighties, Ingram's research sought philosophic as well as pragmatic answers to the issue of where dance belongs in higher education. Ingram's interviews with professors of dance revealed a passionate position regarding the divergent directions dance and physical education departments should take:

If dance is in a physical education department which focuses on the aesthetic and expressive dimensions of movement and not just on the competitive aspect, philosophically dance can exist there. Having now been in a full-fledged dance department separate from physical education for eight years, I have stopped hoping and trying to make a relationship with physical education work. Outside of our roots in human movement, we actually have very little in common. We are after different outcomes, teach very differently, and look at dance very differently. We move for different reasons, we are concerned always with the intrinsic value of how it feels and not just with what is accomplished by the moving. We are appalled by the huge classes of aerobic dance taught by physical education people in which the worst of alignment and movement habits are practiced with energy, speed, and constancy to the damage of many bodies . . . Philosophically, there is no more reason for dance and physical education to be grouped together because they are in the medium of movement than for speech and singing to be grouped together because they are concerned with the medium of human sound (1986, 199–200).

Whiteman's (1991) findings revealed as early as 1986 the need for addressing the serious gap in qualifications for those many dance administrators who tended to learn these roles on the job. Research on management competency in physical education and sport conducted by Paris in 1979 would provide a model for use in the field of dance by others, including Alma Hawkins, a pioneer in dance education and founder of Council of Dance Administrators or CODA (Whiteman 1991).

Precedent exists that applications for tenure of dance faculty are often denied based upon ignorance of the discipline and devaluation of evidence of merit (Wood 1991, 109). In addition, a Damoclean gender sword hangs over the head of women faculty due to traditional prejudicial evaluation of creative work based on female themes or aggressively feminist in nature (Wood 1991, 112–113). Wood persuasively states that

as women, the majority of dance faculty begins the tenure/promotion process from a disadvantaged position. The lack of knowledge about the discipline on the part of faculty from other fields and the resistance to the inclusion of creative endeavors as scholarship combine to place the application of dance faculty in peril. Dance as a discipline must specify standards and methodologies to measure excellence in creative endeavors that reflect the same rigor of judgment applied in other disciplines (1991, 113).

The historic debates within academia regarding why tenure should remain or be abolished reflect deeply held suppositions about quality, content, history, and vision in any college or university. Every tenure appointment has important financial implications for the institution at large. Therefore, it is incumbent for an "underdog" field to put in the necessary footwork in order to prepare strong, cohesive, and viable tenure applications (Wood 1991).

Clemente (1991) points out that justification for many traditional college and university dance education programs could be dependent upon (1) job opportunities in that state upon the completion of dance education degrees, (2) the lack of state mandates for dance education in public schools K–12, (3) the dilemma resulting from the practice of combining dance certification with other subject areas (not including physical education), and (4) state or school district level board of education practices that preclude hiring in dance unless within the physical education subject area.

During the 1990s, serious analysis of the value of dance in higher education began in research circles. This is partially in response to the explosion in technology, including the access to information and experience, which has in itself, revolutionized postsecondary education, the arts, and the scope of commercial and nonprofit employment opportunities. However, veteran professional performers and choreographers analyze the place of dance in higher education through the unique lenses and perspectives of their own years of professional experiences. Broadway dancer and choreographer Tina Paul states,

> The snag to a college education is that your degree doesn't mean "squat" in an audition. A doctor goes to medical school and earns a grade point average that determines which hospital will accept her for an internship and or residency. After that, she can set up shop. Or a high school teacher studies through grad school, passes the certification exam and secures a teaching position. These are wonderful professions, but the salaried appointments largely depend on paperwork, the grades, and the degree. Not so in theatre. No one cares about the degree except as a barometer to the amount of training you have had. They care if a dancer can do the arabesque, the jump, the turn. That's what gets you the job (2003, 58).

Renowned and award-winning choreographer Graciela Daniele discusses her struggle to maintain a sense of self-worth in the face of prevailing attitudes telling her that a diploma was a necessary professional qualification:

> One time I was talking with Joe Papp [artistic director of Public The-
> atre in New York City] and I said that I sometimes feel shy because
> everybody here graduated "this and that," and I don't have that. He
> said, "What are you talking about? In college, people learn what is
> given to them. You learned what was important to you. You read
> yourself. How many languages do you speak?" I said, "Well, four."
> He said, "Did you read Aristotle?" I said, "Yes, of course. I bought
> Aristotle and I didn't like it too much. I don't agree with his ideas
> about women." He laughed and said, "You have a mind of your own.
> You have a universal education that Americans don't have, so why
> should you feel badly?" . . . but inside, it is still intimidating when
> someone has gone to Yale and I have only a high school diploma. But
> it's funny . . . now as I go to speak at Yale and other colleges, I always
> start by saying that I have no academic credits, but I have experience
> (Paul 2003, 58).

Based upon her years of experience in working with emerging young talent, Paul suggests, if possible, the advantages if one is able to combine both academic and professional training opportunities simultaneously:

> A way to get the best of both worlds is to attend one of the colleges or
> universities in New York City. The environment is safer; you will be
> among students from all over the country and away from home for the
> first time and housing is available and more affordable. While getting
> a superb education, you will be in the hub of the action. If you have
> time, you can take classes at the many studios, depending upon the
> school's policy. Since Broadway casting directors, directors, and cho-
> reographers live in New York City, they go to see student productions
> at the performing arts schools more often than their scheduled visits
> elsewhere. By participating simply as a part of your curriculum, you
> are gaining exposure . . . you are here. Casting directors and agents
> can keep an eye on your progress and in auditions, choreographers
> and directors may recognize you (2003, 61).

Despite the myriad advantages that such a societal transformation has afforded every aspect of American culture, economic realities for young and aspiring artists have created an unusual situation and opportunity within the field of dance:

How many young aspiring dancers today who go to New York are able to afford even two daily classes in their professional studies or to find the studio space and professional guidance to try their hand at choreography? In universities across the nation the fact is that the roles of all the arts have become more professionally oriented in recent years as administrators have begun to give recognition to the fine arts in the total educational scheme. Through their expanded functions, colleges and departments of fine arts are in a sense replacing the old music conservatories, dramatic schools, and dance and art academies with their narrowly focused curriculums. The best of the fine arts departments in universities are providing their students with the facilities and faculty expertise that they need to complete their basic professional studies but with the added advantage of being able to make available resources and course offerings in a multitude of other disciplines to stimulate the potential artist (Hayes 1997, 343).

Preparing Students for Careers in Dance-Related Fields

The preceding view of the field and the future opens the doors for inter-disciplinary or double majors to prepare students for careers in dance therapy, teaching, technical theater, dance management, dance notation and reconstruction, sports medicine, arts management, dance writing and research, videography for dance, and music for dance. Topaz points out that although departments are broadening their curricula to include these new course offerings, it is imperative to expand the awareness in students and parents of burgeoning new occupational possibilities:

We try to train our students to be "awake dreamers." Because a lot of students at Loyola come from parental backgrounds in which they are expected to be practical and productive, they tend to abandon their dreams very much too soon. Being an "awake dreamer" means culti-vating the skills that you need, finding out the talents you have, and yet not letting go of your dream of dancing. You have to be able to speak and write, not be a moron about technology, be able to work equipment, and connect to the community. For example, if I wanted to be a Las Vegas showgirl with my four-foot, eleven-inch body, that would be a sleepy dream. We try to keep them awake and planning concretely for careers . . . We are really going into technology in dance, having computerized lighting boards to work with, giving the opportunity to be stage managers and even lighting designers. And we are moving towards having a computerized choreography program like the one Merce Cunningham uses . . . The other thing we concentrate on is the science connected to dance. There are jobs out there for dancers who know about the human body and how it works. Some of our students find employment as rehabilitative people or specialists in dance injury prevention . . . (1994, 64).

Dance programs in postsecondary education in the twenty-first century are positioned to build significant, groundbreaking linkages and affiliations with other academic disciplines within their own institutions. Such alliances will provide education and training that equips students to compete for many newly created jobs in performing and nonperforming sectors. The potential for recognition of dance and its contribution to American culture and society as a whole—nearly one hundred years since the work of H'Doubler—stands to gain immeasurably (Grody 1996).

Summary

The current acceptance of dance in American popular culture has evolved proportionately to the diminishment of negative religious and societal attitudes. Particularly, the evolution of a twenty-first-century paradigm for dance education marks a journey of courageous performers, choreographers, and teachers, who fearlessly challenge the status quo in both aesthetic and physical education. As radical new techniques and physical vocabularies were created and embraced, emphasis shifted to empowering the makers of dance with their own individual movement voices. Traditional artistic hierarchies transformed, and a corresponding shift occurred for the validity of dance education in both K–12 as well as postsecondary institutions. Access and opportunity were now widely afforded and with such also the possibility of a career.

Everyone knows professional dancers must begin training at an early age in order to develop strength and coordination, and to maintain the unnatural degree of flexibility that dancing necessitates. After about ten years of arduous training—often requiring the sacrifice of intellectual pursuits or social activities—the dancer reaches the ideal point of readiness to embark on a professional career. The body is thoroughly trained, yet still fresh enough to withstand the rigors of daily classes, stressful auditions, lengthy rehearsals, and nightly performances. Why then, would a dancer choose to spend these prime performing years— from age nineteen to twenty-one—sitting in math classes, reading literature, writing history papers, conducting science experiments, and dancing only part-time, within the confines of a college or university setting? "Because," suggests Stephan Laurent, "when you take the time to educate the person—not just the body—you end up with a true artist and not simply a technique machine" (Sagolla 1998, 30).

Dance in higher education has gained respect and academic accreditation as barriers of resistant thinking have fallen away in favor of views accepting the arts as essential components of a fully integrated educational experience for persons of all ages or levels of development (Hanna 1999). Today, students and their parents can weigh the pros and cons of going to college, auditioning for professional companies (or their schools), going to New York City without college, or coming to New York City to attend one of the city's many colleges and training schools. The option to train in a postsecondary institution to prepare for a career path in dance depends largely on the unique ability of an institution to deliver a high-caliber comprehensive program. How postsecondary institutions create and implement principles and practices by which such success can be attained comprised the next focus of this study.

Chapter Three

Methodology

Introduction

The rationale, assumptions, and questions that comprised this study must be addressed by a methodology that can answer the overall research question:

> *What are the effective principles and practices that exist*
> *in effective university-level dance programs that sufficiently*
> *prepare students for career paths in dance?*

This chapter will discuss why a qualitative design approach was selected in order to accomplish this end. Areas included in this section are (1) an overview of research methodology or approach, (2) differing assumptions in qualitative versus quantitative research design, (3) type of qualitative design (phenomenological), (4) negotiating the research relationships, (5) selection of participants, (6) data collection procedures, (7) data recording procedures, (8) data analysis procedures, (9) validity and reliability, (10) reporting, and (11) protection of subjects and ethical considerations.

Research Methods

Overview of Research Approach

In order to obtain the data necessary required to formulate a comprehensive comparison of postsecondary institution's curricula for dance education and dance performance in higher education, a qualitative methodology was utilized for the purpose of this investigation in order to address the research question, "What are the effective principles and practices that exist in effective university-level dance programs that sufficiently prepare students for career paths in dance?"

Several key components of qualitative methodology provided an advantage in using this approach in the study. It has been determined that a qualitative study design would be effective for the following reasons:

- In this study there was no established priori theory or hypothesis as to what would be stated in quantitative studies (Babbie 1990).
- In this study the data that emerged was descriptive, and the data was primarily in words rather than numbers (Berg 1998).
- In this study the focus was on the participants' perceptions of and experiences [in their dance education programs] and the ways in which they made sense [of their career paths] in light of these (Fraenkel and Wallen 1996; Locke, et al 1987; Merriam 1988).
- In this study the researcher included not only the focus on the product (determining the success rates of the programs in the study) but also on an evaluative process that provided an opportunity for the participants to analyze, interpret, and come to their own individual conclusions independently of the overall findings suggested by the study (Patton 1990).

Differing Assumptions in Qualitative and Quantitative Designs

Each design paradigm holds different methodological assumptions (Firestone 1987; Guba and Lincoln 1988; McCracken 1988; Creswell 1994). In a quantitative model, the assumption is that reality is singularly objective and detached from the researcher. In this qualitative study, however, the assumption was that reality is subjective and consists of a multiplicity of perceptions on dance, dance education, and the perceptions and definitions of professional career possibilities held by the participants as well as the researcher (Bogdan and Bilken 1982).

The assumption in the quantitative model dictates that the researcher maintains distance and independence from that being researched. In this study, however, the assumption was made that interaction between the participants (who are dance professors) and the researcher (who is a choreographer, dance teacher, and arts education advocate) played a key role in the process. Subjectivity was essential since the terminology used in the profession is domain specific.

Unbiased, values-free research is the axiological assumption in a quantitative model (Babbie 1998). However, in this study it was necessary to employ a qualitative model in order for a biased and values-rich pool to inform the analysis of the research question by both the participants and the researcher. The research question itself is a natural outgrowth of this researcher's own experiences as the cofounder of a non-profit organization comprised of a professional company of dancers and a thriving studio for students of all levels of interest, talent, aspiration, and racial and socioeconomic background.

For both participants and readers of the study to gain a contextual framework for the research question, it was also necessary to present the worldview that the researcher brought. The worldview of the researcher is presented through the lens of an experienced educator and administrator, who has counseled scores of parents and their children regarding the possibility of continued dance education at the college or university level. This will be discussed in further detail in the section entitled "Researcher Positionality."

Rhetorical assumptions in a quantitative model characterize the language of research as formal and impersonal (Fowler 1993). In the qualitative model of this study, an informal and personal voice in the research language was employed in order to maximize the potential for clarity of response and articulation of thought by participants whose data were recorded through a variety of data collection activities.

"Collecting information from a diverse range of individuals and settings using a variety of methods" (Denzin 1970) is known as triangulation. Triangulation is critical to validity of a qualitative study because it supports a finding by showing that independent measures of it agree with it or, at least, do not contradict it. Triangulation is a way to get to the findings—by seeing or hearing multiple instances of the data from different sources and through different collection methods (Miles and Huberman 1994). The general principle of triangulation was used during the data collection, which included the following methods:

- Recorded and transcribed personal telephone interviews
- Interview guide (see appendix B)
- Written interviews via handwritten accounts and sent via fac-simile or electronic mail
- Review of historical documents, including university mission statements, catalogs, factual university Web site pages, and other informational sources documents

Finally, the methodological assumptions within a quantitative model—static designs seeking cause and effect—do not naturally lend themselves to this kind of study. However, the methodological assumptions within a qualitative model—patterns and an overarching design within a context—provided this research study a process suitable to discerning answers that the questions in this investigation ultimately posed.

Type of Qualitative Design: Phenomenological

The intention of this study was to determine the effective principles and practices that exist in effective university-level dance programs. The philosophical underpinnings and pedagogical content intrinsic to the research question are issues that must be fearlessly asked and answered by teachers and educators in any dance program. What does it mean to *sufficiently* prepare students? As well, prospective parents who are about to invest four years of finances and other resources attempt in their own ways to determine how each school sufficiently equips its graduates to enter the workforce with confidence. It was hoped, therefore, that through nonrandom purposeful sampling or "information-rich case sampling" (Patton 1990) of those who teach at the college level a view of their life worlds could be gained. Thus, the theoretical orientation of this study is phenomenological (Idhe 1986).

> Phenomenology refers to the description of one or more individuals' consciousness and experience of a phenomenon . . . The purpose of phenomenological research is to obtain a view into your research participants' life-worlds and to understand their personal meanings (what it means to them) constructed from their life experiences (Johnson and Christensen 2000, 315).

As a researcher, this investigation was entered into with no preconceived theory. While this investigation did not specifically fall within the realm of grounded theory it, nonetheless, shares a common characteristic, for this study dealt with the relationship between data and "validated statements of relationship between concepts during the research process" (Strauss and Corbin 1998, 5). This researcher was engaged in an *ongoing* process of engagement with the data. The heart of grounded theory is data "systematically gathered and analyzed through the research process" (Strauss and Corbin 1998, 12).

This study gathered data primarily through detailed narrative accounts from the participants. This researcher intended to interpret meaning from these anecdotal statements collected through the various data collection methods previously described. Therefore, the design being used to answer the research question represents an interpretive, phenomenological approach.

> Interpretivists of all types insist that researchers are not more "detached" from their objects of study than are their informants. Researchers, they argue, have their own understandings, their own convictions, their own conceptual orientations; they, too, are members of a particular culture at a specific historical moment. Also they will be undeniably affected by what they heard and observed in the field, often in unnoticed ways (Miles & Huberman 1994, 8).

Values and biases shape this researcher's experiences. These are based in experiences as a college dance student, professional performer, choreographer, teacher, arts educator, community activist, and administrator of a nonprofit dance company. Unifying these experiences is a personal belief that the arts are vital to human experience. The underpinnings of this work are embodied in the conviction that dance is a means of deeply emotional and spiritual personal expression as well as a medium for bringing communities together for social interaction, celebration, worship, and aesthetic nourishment.

For this study, these biases had sufficient controls in place. Among them were the utilizing of independent experts and resources to assist the researcher in developing the interview questions. Procedures (such as informed consent from the participants) were put in place to ensure that data-collection activities were explicated and justified as appropriate. One analysis component of the study also included utilizing outside consultants from industries outside the arts or arts education in which participants might have been employed.

The many questions and subquestions of this study were best asked and answered within the phenomenological approach. In this design, a rubric was suggested through a holistic view enabling the analysis to provide an emphasis on "lived experience" that assists in locating meaning for processes, structures, and events in participants' lives (Miles and Huberman 1994, 10).

Researcher Positionality

The journey of this researcher to a worldview that informed the desire to conduct this study is grounded in a lifelong fascination with and appreciation of two personal core values in good teaching—intelligence and dedication. In over twenty years working as a dancer, administrator, and arts educator an enriching spectrum of people, experiences, and circumstances have combined to create a personal standard that measures integrity and excellence pertaining to the classroom, the studio, the rehearsal hall, and the stage.

Motives and assumptions within to the researcher's worldview are linked to her initial training as a dancer. Local studios in the area of Boston, Massachusetts, afforded an excellent technical foundation for entrance into the School of Hartford Ballet following high school graduation in 1978. In addition to performing classical repertoire in the corps, the researcher pursued an interest in studying the pedagogical techniques of ballet by participating in a two-year teacher-training program jointly administered by the school and Connecticut College. The consequences of a major knee injury led to a period of physical recuperation and rehabilitation in South Florida. During this period, the researcher underwent a period of reflection and personal evaluation of the options and means for achieving success and satisfaction in a dance profession.

Cofounding, managing, and continuing to dance professionally for fifteen years with a nationally recognized contemporary company Klein Dance provided the necessary experience and tools in arts management to also successfully administer a school for pre-K through adult with an enrollment of 250 students. Key to developing the reputation of this company and school has been a careful, considered process for identifying excellent teachers and for maintaining a consistently high-caliber of instruction.

The criteria for evaluating the teachers and studio are based upon this researcher's belief that excellence in dance education includes an intuitive understanding of the necessary balance between process and product, as well as between intuition and pedagogy (Hanna 1999). Beyond mere dedication, assisting each student in reaching his/her full potential specifically involves recognizing talent, defining the upper limits of expectation and accomplishment, articulating the means toward achieving those goals, and then providing the technical tools and opportunities for this to occur. Finally, true attainment of both technique and artistry also requires a mentoring relationship between student and teacher—that singular, cherished, often-indefinable symbiosis that lies at the very heart of learning (Franklin 1996).

The challenges in developing the artistic and educational signature of the company and school paralleled those often found in many postsecondary dance education programs, including at Palm Beach Atlantic University (PBAU) where the researcher is currently employed as director of dance. Enlightened administrators at this liberal arts–based school have provided the means necessary to offer an accredited major in dance—including history, theory, and pedagogy—where until 1999 there was only a scattering of credits available in ballet, tap, and jazz.

This researcher's scholarly interest lies in gaining a deeper knowledge and understanding of strengths and weaknesses of other dance programs in higher education around the country. There has been strong encouragement from PBAU administrators to define a vision and strategy for building an even stronger department of dance within the school of music and fine arts. As part of a quality initiative, faculty members receive strong support and financial underwriting for scholarly research that advances both the mission of the school as well as making contributions to the individual fields of research. The core educational and institutional values shared between this researcher and PBAU administrators frame an identity of mutual interest for conducting a research study from which the findings can be applied to the school in developing its own comprehensive program while also making a larger contribution to the under-researched field of dance education in postsecondary institutions. According to statistics set forth by the National Dance Education Organization, the majority of research studies that have been done in the dance field have been published only as recently as 1980.

Negotiating the Research Relationship

Despite searches of the literature, to this researcher's knowledge, no pilot studies exist for this research idea or specific question. Interest in this study originated early in the researcher's tenure at PBAU, a Christian university that had not yet offered any type of comprehensive, accredited dance program. Realizing that years of experience as an arts educator, administrator, and performer could be invaluable when applied to the development of an entire dance curriculum, this researcher approached PBAU administrators with the idea of linking a dissertation topic to the school's desire for an accredited program. The study, therefore, has had reciprocal benefits. The university assisted in costs associated with undertaking this study while being able to benefit from the engagement of the researcher in the investigative process.

Selection of Participants

Through the review of related literature for information on existing college- and university-level dance education programs, the researcher has discovered that there are multiple foci across a wide number of schools. Although most schools claim the ability to equip students with the necessary tools to make dance a viable career choice, this researcher needed to identify faculty at schools with distinctly different concentrations.

Johnson and Christensen (2000) suggest that a collective case study may be used to study multiple cases in one overall research study in an effort to gain greater insights on similarities and differences (p. 208). In this study, eight faculty members from eight schools were selected and were identified through electronic mail inquiries, informal conversations, and professional dance organization affiliations and, based upon the quality of their programs, their focus and concentration, distinctness of individual curriculum, differing geographic locations, differences in demographics, and the researcher's access to them. This may represent a biased perspective on the researcher's part as it pertains to the ability to collect and manage data based on sufficient access to institutions or individuals in certain parts of the country. Verbal commitment from key faculty at each school was gained. Further refinement of the selection process and final determination of participating institutions took place with the assistance of the researcher's dissertation chairman, committee members, faculty, and other professional colleagues.

The dance program in each of the schools that were considered evolved within a uniquely derived context of each geographic area. The influence of these strong cultural considerations is reflected in the course offerings, enrollment, composition of faculty, and affiliations of the program with other local, state, regional, and national organizations and institutions.

Collection and Recording of Data

A variety of instrumentation measures such as open-ended questionnaires and interview techniques were necessary in order to collect and record data pertinent to the research questions and subquestions. Dexter (1970) states that

> no one should plan or finance an entire study in advance with the expectation of relying chiefly upon interviews for data unless the interviewers have enough relevant background to be sure that they can make sense out of interview conversations or unless there is a reasonable hope of being able to hang around or in some way observe so as to learn what it is meaningful and significant to ask (1970, 17).

Written interviews were combined and/or followed up with personal interviews conducted via phone or in person. Interviews are thought to be powerful instruments for exploring complicated emotions and experiences (MacLaren 1980). A preinterview guide was provided to respondents in order to prepare them by framing the questions. Each personal interview was sixty to ninety minutes in length and was audiotaped. The service of a transcriber was required at times.

> The purpose of interviewing is to find out what is in and on someone else's mind. The purpose of open-ended interviewing is not to put things in someone else's mind (for example, the interviewer's preconceived categories for organizing the world) but to access the perspective of the person being interviewed (Patton 1990, 278).

Journal notes containing additional basic information, such as "descriptions of what have been observed" (Patton 1990, 239), as well as impressions and speculation about the participants and the settings were taken as well. Memoing was completed before and after each interview and throughout the process of interpretation and analysis. As Maxwell

(1996) states, one should "regularly write memos while doing data analysis to facilitate reflection and insight" (p. 11). Ongoing data analysis was conducted simultaneously with data collection, transcription of interviews, and narrative journal writing. Themes were identified within cases through axial coding.

> Axial coding helps the researcher transform concepts into categories and organizes the categories. The researcher looks to see what kinds of things were mentioned by the participant many times (what themes appeared across the interviews). The researcher looks for possible relationships among the categories in the data (Johnson and Christensen 2000, 336).

QSR NVivo 2.0, a highly specialized and advanced software program was utilized as a strategy to handle the coding for data analysis. As within-case themes and patterns emerged, creative data displays were developed in order to facilitate systemic analysis.

Validity/Reliability

Maxwell's work (1996) provides a structure to apply in order to ensure internal validity to the study. This includes descriptive validity (what was said); interpretive validity (what it meant to the people involved); theoretical validity (concepts and their relationships used to explain actions and meanings); and evaluative validity (judgments of the worth or value of actions and meanings). The researcher worked closely with the committee chair, Dr. William Leary, to ensure the integrity of this aspect of the work.

Regular review and checks by members of the researcher's committee were necessary to ensure that the integrity of the participants' words had been maintained throughout the process of interpretation and analysis. In addition, adherence to data collection and interpretation procedures was maintained through abiding with the existing literature on qualitative research. With this system of self-monitoring, it is anticipated that there should be a strong viability for replication of this kind of study.

Participant feedback and the verification of this researcher's interpretations and conclusions were conducted. Feedback from the participants was essential to achieving interpretive validity. Member checks were used in order to clarify any areas of miscommunication (Lincoln and Guba 1985). In a member check, the person being researched is requested to examine rough drafts of writing where his/her actions are featured. The person is then asked to review the material for accuracy and palatability. The person then may be encouraged to provide an alternate interpretation if warranted (Johnson and Christensen 2000).

Transferability of this data and the conclusions drawn constituted the external validity of the research. Following the conclusion of this investigation, this researcher was curious as to the response of the participating schools to the specific principles and practices that the study assesses as effective in contributing to successful employment of graduating students from the respective dance programs. Of further interest will be how the rubric may (or may not) be applied by Palm Beach Atlantic University in addressing its expressed need for a viable dance program within the school of music and fine arts.

Reporting

The findings of this research were reported in subjective as well as objective voice, presenting and preserving the participants' words with the statistical information as well. In order to develop the rubric, the words from the participants were filtered through this researcher's specific lens, with the intention of discovering the most promising principles and practices that can contribute to a high success rate of employment among students graduating from the dance programs in the study.

Protection of Subjects and Ethical Considerations

To ensure the confidentiality of the respondents, pseudonyms were used to identify the participants' words in the transcriptions and final document. Student, faculty, alumni, and any additional participants were protected through the signing of consent forms and/or confidentiality agreements. This process was overseen by the institutional review board. It is not anticipated that the questions in the interviews may have caused any concern, insecurity, or discomfort for the respondents. In fact, it is hoped that the participants in the dissertation investigation have acquired a sense of genuine inclusion and positive contribution to the focus, goals, and results of this study.

Summary

This chapter was written merely as a brief overview for the overall research plan. Several functional definitions as well as clarifications of procedures and structures were determined to adequately carry out this study. Determination of specific elements of these mechanisms grew out of ongoing discussions and meetings with committee members and consultations with Dr. Leary.

While this study strove to be comprehensive, it did not pretend or attempt to be exhaustive. As the phenomenological research design, development of instruments, and data-collection techniques were refined during the course of the investigation, it was hoped that they might, ultimately, serve as an investigative model for use in future studies.

> Are we systematically looking for proof of the positive effects of a dance education, or are we continuing to rely on anecdotal evidence in making the case for curriculum-based, sequential, dance education in our schools? Is there a dance equivalent to the "Mozart Effect," perhaps an "Isadora Effect"? Should we, like our friends the scientists, project the next steps in the experimental sequence? Is there something to be learned from the scientific method in this regard? (Hagood 2000, 27).

It is hoped that access to these findings by members of the college/university dance communities at a national level will provide a new contribution to the field by introducing a rubric into the lexicon that will serve as a catalyst for interacademic dialogue. Through this research, perhaps, others may also travel along similar paths of inquiry and investigation. A significant outcome to be gained might then be that together, rather than in isolation, educators might achieve greater success in strengthening and advocating for the integrity and position of dance in colleges and universities in America.

Chapter Four

Data and Analysis

Introduction

Chapter 4 presents a model for the way that participants in this study express their concerns for the justification, stability, and future of dance at the postsecondary level. The model was conceptualized with the goal of eliciting information through asking questions divided into five categories. Responses were grouped according to codes outlining specific observations from key faculty participants at each selected school. In some cases, data could not be used since it may have threatened the confidentiality agreement by making participants identifiable to the reader. This element of the research conforms to the research protocol requirements and confidentiality agreement. Data reduction required quotes and stories taken out of context from each participant's transcript and files to be coded through NVivo software.

The qualitative data results are analyzed in this chapter primarily through a contextualizing strategy. The purpose in employing this method is to look for relationships that connect the responses, seeking a context for a coherent whole (Maxwell 1996).

Working with the data collected from participants, a pattern emerged as to how the respondents engaged themselves in the question of validity and quality pertaining to criteria and standards for career preparation in dance. By looking with cases, evidence was provided to develop categories and themes. Responses to the questions posed in the study crossed institutional lines and contexts. The coded data actually revealed the commonality of issues and conflicts facing all the educators in this study.

Therefore, the findings are presented in this chapter as a synthesis of responses from among the entire pool of respondents rather than subdivided into smaller subsets of data.

Five Categories of Consideration

Determining the best principles and practices of dance programs entails matching aspirations and hopes of students and parents with the missions and goals of prospective institutions and their programs. The questions in this study posed to the faculty respondents regarding their own individual programs reflect the important concerns of the college-bound family.

Years of experience in facilitating this often subjective, if not "hit or miss" process, with such families has provided this researcher with knowledge of the many questions consistently raised in attempting to select "the right school." These concerns, along with issues raised in informal discussions with other professional dance educators, led this researcher to compile an initial list of forty questions pertaining to criteria for determining the quality and suitability of a program.

In order to create a data-collection process that was both thorough as well as participant friendly, these questions were reduced to nineteen and then grouped into categories reflecting the distinct areas of mutual interest between schools and prospective enrollees. Each category focuses on eliciting information about a specific aspect of the education process:

- Attitude—the expectation held by students and parents; what are these expectations based upon?
- Knowledge—what is the body of information to be taught and the pedagogical approach to doing so?
- Skills—the practical tools with which the students will leave.
- Behavior—the way the student implements his/her training vocationally or in other situations.

A fifth category of consideration and background was created to gather information about the individual participants in the study. The interview questions were then grouped into these categories in order for the answers to create snapshots of an institution's career readiness preparation criteria and standards for career paths in dance.

Background of Participants

Participants in the study represent a wide range of experiences and backgrounds. All are educators, yet each has worn or continues to wear the hats of artist, administrator, and/or advocate. Gender and ethnicity were not considerations for the purpose of this study. Eight participants representing eight schools were selected through purposeful sampling and interviewed. The participants consisted of a group of eight females ranging in age from twenty-five years old to sixty-five years old. Details on all participants are listed under their respective school listings in the following pages.

Confidentiality of all respondents was assured through the assigning of the following pseudonyms borrowed from dance terminology:

School A: Sissonne
School B: Allegro
School C: Jeté
School D: Barre
School E: En L' Aire
School F: Dehors
School G: De Chat
School H: Cheval

School A is located in the extreme southeastern area of the United States. It is the youngest of the schools in this study yet has the largest enrollment and annual operating budget. It opened in 1972 and offers more than 190 baccalaureate, master's, and doctoral degree programs in 19 colleges and schools. The school currently consists of 34,000 students, 1,100 full-time faculty, and 95,000 alumni placing it among the nation's 30 largest colleges and universities. The student body is a microcosm of the city in which it is located, with nearly 70 percent of student enrollment from minority groups. Tuition costs (housing is not available for undergraduate students) annually are approximately $2,700 for state students and $12,000 for out-of-state students. One respondent was interviewed from this school:

- **Sissonne**—married, middle-aged female (tenured associate professor/dance department chair) with a doctorate of arts

School B was founded in 1874 as a coed, residential, four-year private liberal arts college in the upper Midwest, approximately forty-five minutes from a large metropolitan area. In its long history, annual enrollment has grown to over 3,000 students, and its nationally recognized academic divisions provide thirty-eight bachelor of arts and four bachelor of music degree programs at the undergraduate level. The full-time faculty is comprised of 355 members, its student/faculty ratio is at 12:1, and the average class size hovers around twenty-one. The school is affiliated with the Evangelical Lutheran Church, and the student body demographics strongly reflect a Norwegian, Lutheran heritage. Annual comprehensive fees for tuition, room, and board are approximately $27,000. One respondent was interviewed from this school:

- **Allegro**—single, middle-aged woman (tenured associate professor/dance department chair) with a PhD in dance.

School C has retained a rather small enrollment with 3,275 students and 189 full-time faculty since its founding in 1871. It is located in the heart of the Midwest on a 280-acre campus in a town of 5,000 residents. There are 189 full-time faculty members. Its student/faculty ratio is 13:1, and the average class size is 24. The school is private, coeducational, and affiliated with the United Methodist Church and places strong emphasis on its excellent networking connections with employers. Annual tuition plus room and board equal approximately $18,000.
One respondent was selected from this school:

- **Jeté**—married, middle-aged woman (associate professor/director of dance) with a doctorate in education

School D is a private, liberal arts college related to the United Methodist Church and located in the southeastern area of the United States. This small college was founded in 1854 and currently has an enrollment of 239 men and 377 women. It offers bachelor of arts degrees in many fields and has forty-five full-time faculty. The fifty-eight-acre suburban campus has a student-faculty ratio of 12:1. This school is accredited by the National Association of Schools of Music. Annual tuition costs for undergraduate students are approximately $18,000. One respondent was chosen from this school:

- **Barre**—married, middle-aged woman (assistant professor/ coordinator of dance program) with a masters of fine arts in dance.

School E, a college in the northeastern part of the country, admits young women only. This school has a dance student body of less than two hundred students per year and has both national and international students. Students come from twenty different states and fifteen different countries. The faculty expresses a desire to open a door to a lifetime in the arts by sharing a philosophy between the visual and performing arts departments of the school. One respondent was chosen from this school:

- **En L' Aire**—single, middle-aged woman (tenured professor/dance department chair) with a masters of fine arts in dance

School F is a comprehensive public university in the southern part of the United States with an enrollment of approximately 25,000 graduate and undergraduate students in eight different colleges. This school does not have a program offering dance as a major field of study, but incorporates its dance courses into the theater program. This school was selected because of the strength of its theater program and the fact that the dance courses offered strongly support the dance/theater performers who aspire to work in the commercial sector. One respondent from this school was interviewed:

- **Dehors**—single, middle-aged woman (tenured full professor/director of the dance program within the department of theatre) with a PhD in theater history

School G is a northwestern public university with specialized, advanced level arts programs in music, dance, visual arts, and theater supported by a strong academic program. With an overall enrollment of over 32,000 campuswide, the dance program at this school provides intensive training in different styles and techniques of ballet, modern, and jazz dance with an emphasis on a personalized atmosphere. One respondent from this school was interviewed:

- **De Chat**—single, middle-aged woman (dance professor/co-ordinator of dance program) with a masters of fine arts in dance

School H is located in the north central region of the United States, opening in 1868 and offering more than 150 different programs of study in eight colleges and schools. The school currently consists of 38,291 students, 1,908 full-time faculty and a staff of 5,500, placing it also among the nation's 30 largest colleges and universities. The location of this school is on 1,454 acres near a major metropolitan area. Tuition costs annually are approximately $7,000 for state students and $16,000 for out-of-state students. Three different theaters spaces seat 1,750 to 16,500 people. The dance program offers bachelor of fine arts and master of fine arts degrees in dance for the preparation of professional choreographers, performers, and studio teachers. One respondent from this school was chosen for the study:

- **Cheval**—single, young woman (part-time assistant professor of dance) with a masters of fine arts in dance performance

The following is a presentation of the researcher's findings for this study.

Attitude

The disposition or predisposition toward pursuing a life in the profession of dance is shaped by personal ambition as well as external influences. As stated by the respondents in this study, the goals and intentions for actions leading to jobs reflect certain common core beliefs and circumstances. Perceptions of success were also reflective of these as well.

In agreement that striving to achieve a career in dance is equally a demanding mental pursuit as well as a physical challenge; participants consistently spoke of various personal habits, interests, and values as indicators of the potential for success in a student. Focus, self-discipline, and time management—all of which are generated qualities from within—were cited regularly as necessary practices in this category.

Several participants point out that the field of dance requires ongoing—in fact, daily—training. Therefore, an attitude can only be healthy and useful if it is grounded in an awareness of patience and process. Barre describes, "Focus on short-term goals to achieve long-term goals" (coding file, sec. 1.2. para 30). For En L' Aire, the student must be "willing to understand the repetition and patience in process" (coding file, sec. 0, para 29–31). Jeté says,

> Many talented kids have come through the program but have not succeeded. Are you willing to work three part-time jobs to pay your rent in New York and still have the energy to go to auditions, take classes and make phone calls? How long are you willing to do that? One year? Three years? Five years? How do you want to live until you get your big break? (coding file, sec 1, para 21).

Rejection, as a part of performing careers, is a reality for which students must be prepared. Respondents mention inner, innate qualities that can fortify a student with resilience. But these same qualities also bring intrinsically holistic benefits. De Chat states, "A healthy view of self . . . the physical discipline should be to achieve grounding and self-awareness" (coding file, sec. 0, para 38). Sissonne at School A describes a particular dilemma where a student lacked focus and motivation. The student was unequipped to deal with a future of rejection due to a lack of inner focus, concentration, and ability to follow through:

> Currently we have a senior in our program. She transferred in from another school as a late sophomore. She was extremely flighty and unfocused and tended to be influenced by whoever she may be hanging with at the moment. She showed no real interest in learning and was extremely insecure. She participated in the building consortium class and it seems that the course really inspired her, brought her out of her daze and now she is involved in several community-based arts programs as well as directing and producing an upcoming fundraiser called Project Refire—Dance for Food. She is raising monies for the hungry in our country as well as a community in another country. She has earned a free plane ticket to another country and will be going there to help deliver food and assist in helping the community construct pipes for water to grow their own food source. She has made a one hundred and eighty degree turnaround—very impressive. Now she has direction in her life, is very talented in teaching in community-based programs and has grown in her sense of self-esteem (Sissonne transcript file p. 4, lines 149–162).

Here social consciousness intersected with the art form to generate new attitudes of passion and dedication with the outcome that of a committed young artist/activist now on a successful track in a nontraditional dance career path.

De Chat stresses to her students to "be open to the limitless possibilities that dance plays in social and cultural dynamics" stating,

> My vision about dance [at school G] differs from my current colleagues. I do share the same appreciation for aesthetic quality and maturity for dance as they do. However, with regard to training dancers; I look at a cross-section of dance makers in West Africa, Butoh, and the former Mudra, who have a global view of dance, their training, and their approach to life through dance . . . in diversifying the art form, I think it will save the art form, not diffuse it (transcript file, p. 1, lines 37–42).

Shaping an attitude that includes a global context for dance is considered an essential responsibility by this educator.

Sissonne considers all the above qualities as essential and admirable but equally applicable to many other academic pursuits. She states,

> The critical issue for me . . . is that dancers really look at and understand dance as "structured" human movement behavior [to quote Adrienne Kepler and other dance anthropologists and ethnologists] and that this structured human movement behavior occurs within a cultural context and that it is very important that dancers understand that all dance comes from a culture and is an ethnic form too. We often don't remember this is in the training of dancers, particularly in the conservatory training, and that essentially means that there are so many different possibilities as to what functions dance has and the role it plays in culture . . . We are living in a shrinking world, particularly for dancers that live in Houston, Miami, Los Angeles, where [previously] the minority culture is all of the sudden the majority. Afghanistan is in our backyard. Iraq is in our living room. I believe that cultivating a global perspective in dance is a way in which we can foster intercultural understanding. This is critical to a dancer's education . . . We can serve ourselves as dancers and society in a much more in-depth and comprehensive way. A dancer must be equipped for this world. One of the ways to equip them in dance is this window . . . and to really understand that. Within that, the dancer can find his or her own place. What are they good at? What expresses their particular uniqueness or passion? (transcript file, p. 2, lines 50–81).

Sissonne's opinion is a striking departure in content and tone from those of other respondents.

When considering fostering attitudes among students, two respondents reflected on how their own dispositions toward the profession were influenced by external circumstances. They realize that incentive to pursue dance administration was entirely absent from their original college training:

> When I began to teach [at school E] twenty-two years ago, I was at the end of my performing career, and I was focused on the task of being the best educator I could be. Having been the chief administrator of a regional dance company, with which I performed, I came to the job with administrative experience that included budget planning, grant writing, scheduling of rehearsals and performances, and staff selection (En L'Aire transcript file, p. 1, lines 36–42).

Jeté at school C responds to this issue:

> After the second child was born, I was looking for career stability. Moving around every couple of years was getting old. I needed a terminal degree in order to have that in the world of higher education . . . I had been advised that an EdD was not the most respected degree, and if I really wanted a degree, I should go for a PhD and I did. I wanted no one telling me my degree was not good enough this time. I majored in higher education administration, figuring I would be in an administrative position in higher education eventually. I minored in Women in America in the Nineteenth Century. This was because I teach dance history and wanted a broader political and social views as it relates to the arts. The degree took me nine years to complete (transcript file, p. 4, lines 180–188).

Knowledge: Curriculum and Instruction

Curriculum and instruction ("instruction" meaning the course content and the pedagogical practices by which information is imparted) are at the heart of academic program accreditation. Accreditation intentionally measures if and how well an institution executes its goals and objectives. In fact, accreditation is a quality compliance audit, a periodic certification of standards. Accreditation does not endorse nor recommend new directions or reform. In postsecondary dance, program designs are modeled, developed, and approved by the accrediting organization, National Association of Schools of Dance.

The findings of this study indicate a uniformity of opinion acknowledging that a foundation of solid technique is the axis around which all other academic criteria must be considered. Participants state that physical competencies within the ballet, modern, and jazz vocabularies are essential neuromotor skills without which one could not be considered "ready" to compete in a performance-based career. Each institution offers syllabi with progressive graded instruction in these three forms: ballet, modern, and jazz. However, participants feel that from that base of physical technique are considerable points of departure regarding what classes or courses should constitute essential core curriculum versus peripheral offerings. Some peripheral offerings might include world dance forms, musical theater choreography, and dance somatics. Each respondent expresses a strong position about what makes certain courses vital and relevant. The opinions are based upon his/her view of the needs of the student in relation to the respondent's perception of an ever-evolving workforce. Clearly imbedded in these opinions are the influences of the respondent's own training and experience, as well as the influencing factors of the geographic location for each institution.

Curriculum is also influenced by determining a prevailing baseline of knowledge among students in the incoming freshmen classes. A highly competitive audition process is often used in conservatories or professional programs to determine admissions, scholarships, and placement levels. While an audition process is mandatory at the schools in this study, it is not intended to exclude students from pursuing a dance major. States Sissonne, "The question implies selection and/or discrimination. It is assumed that background would be a quality high school education—but not always!" (transcript file, p. 2, lines 66–68).

Jeté indicates the need for the inclusion of dance in all public school K–12 curriculums in order to level the playing field for all applicants.

> There are only about seven arts magnet schools in the state. If a school other than a magnet school has a dance unit in their [*sic*] curriculum, it will very likely be taught by someone who had not majored in dance but majored in physical education or elementary education (transcript file, p. 3, lines 97–101).

Sissonne, also at school A, agrees, "The audition process represents a traditional sense of standard, but is really a kind of 'passage.' Most do not come here with professional goals" (coding file, sec. 1.6, para 45). Jeté's program at school C welcomes all students, "We offer only a minor, so we accept a variety of backgrounds, including none (men!). We tailor classes to their technique" (coding file, sec. 1, para 55).

Respondents consider the personal relationship between a teacher and a student to be at the heart of instruction and pedagogy. Jeté's perceptive analysis of the following situation reveals the empathetic and nurturing aspect inherent in a holistic approach to teaching.

I have a specific student in mind, but it is also a general problem I face with students coming from a studio background. A student enrolled here, having at least ten years of experience from the studio in her hometown. Her school had been very involved with competitions, had traveled extensively to these competitions and had many trophies. So, this individual felt she was a very competent dancer. After all, she learned the routines and had competed in many competitions. Upon enrolling in technique classes here at the university, she found herself to be lacking in the technical elements of dance. She didn't have to begin at the beginning, she really had to dump old information and learn new habits which took more work. This was very disheartening for the student because after all this performance experience, she wasn't cast in school shows at the university. I don't know if anyone corrected her at her studio, but from what I've gleaned, they mainly worked on competition material with no "how to" input. I think for this student and myself, the transformation began in the brain. She had to unlearn patterns and not assume anything. She could have told us all that we just didn't know what we were doing, and that she had trophies and so she must be a great dancer. The first battle was her emotional struggle to accept she needed to learn more. Initially, she had no notion of control, turnout, placement, etc. I'm not sure she had any kind of kinesthetic connection. She had to become "aware." It took about two years for any kind of progress to show, but gradually it did. It was a willingness on her part to accept that she needed work and patience on the part of her instructors. Sometimes we all despaired. Eventually, persistence on her part and her teachers' parts began to pay off. There was no "one" moment, just a long journey (transcript follow-up file, p. 1, lines 16–39).

The faculty members seek to assess specific personal or artistic qualities of incoming students as a way of anticipating compatibility with both
the curriculum and individual teaching styles of the faculty. These attributes might include "open-mindedness, willingness to look at different
ways of learning and teaching" (Barre coding file section 1.12, para 50).
Barre looks for "a strong desire to dance and to share that desire with
others" (section 1.2, para 47). Allegro agrees, adding that "the more
opportunity and curiosity they bring, the better they do in our program"
(coding file, sec. 0, para 48).

At school E, En L' Aire embraces a philosophy of working with
students at both ends of the spectrum:

> Open to all levels—welcomed! [But] for advanced incoming students,
> I [do particularly] look for clean barre work, clear understanding of
> basic ballet and modern terminology, open to all forms of dance, no
> mannerisms, musicality, expression, clean lines and the ability to learn
> phrases quickly (En L' Aire coding file, sec. 0, para 52).

While students in all programs take the fundamental studio work in
ballet, modern, and jazz as mentioned previously, most schools supple-
ment these courses with dance history as well as a composition or choreography class. Also, six of the eight programs required a course in kinesiology or other another type of movement modality (Pilates, fitness, or
somatics). Three of the schools required an ethnic or world dance class.
One school required music theory.

With the exception of school D, each institution enhances its own
departmental curriculum and instruction through ongoing efforts to create meaningful collaborations with other disciplines on campus.

> Our department makes a point of interaction with other disciplines on
> campus. We have one faculty member that [sic] is half music and half
> musical theatre. Part of her role is to act as a liaison between the two
> departments. We try to avoid the traditional turf wars. When we have
> various artists on campus, we notify other departments and offer semi-
> nars and master classes to specific departments on the campus at large.
> Our guest instructor in Alexander Technique works with faculty, the
> secretarial staff, and students from all departments on campus. Open
> lines of communication help. This is a small school and generally ev-
> eryone knows everyone else (Jeté transcript file, p. 5, lines 212–214).

Another example of fostering synergy is related by Cheval at school H:

> The dance department and the architecture department collaborated for the opening of a new building. A group of dancers did a site-specific performance in several locations of the building. This was a successful collaboration because it enabled the dancers to perform in a location that was atypical and as a result required a redefinition of the parameters of a performance and performance space. It was beneficial for the spectators and architecture students for similar reasons. Additionally, it opened peoples' minds, looking at alternate uses for spaces and enabling them to view a dance performance from many angles and perspectives (transcript file, p. 3, lines 116–122).

An entire rethinking of departmental mission at school A resulted in a broad curriculum reform. In this program, dance studies are now an integral part of Latin-American and Caribbean cultural studies. Entitled Dance within Disciplines, this broadly-based educational initiative encompasses extensive interdisciplinary cooperation and resources. Requirements in this program major now include the following courses: expressing culture and arts of the African diaspora, the cultural mass in the Americas, critical issues in intercultural understanding, and building community with the arts.

> [The purpose is to] make dance education culturally and pragmatically relevant to the diverse ethnic composition of the student population and the community while introducing dance as an important element in studies (Sissonne coding file, sec. 1.6, para 39).

It is necessary to recall that school A is a public institution and reflects the diversity of its urban setting with a student enrollment that is 49 percent Hispanic and 15 percent African American. The Latin American and Cuban "minority" is the majority. The program at the school has responded to the obvious need to reach out to the underserved urban population in the metropolitan area via an increased emphasis on outreach and community service initiatives that are actually embedded in the dance program curriculum. Dance majors are required to fulfill six credits of outreach service related to specific career goals. A particularly innovative aspect of this component is that students are advised in career interest groups and taught team-learning skills to be applied to specific projects in the community settings. The student is evaluated on his/her problem-solving ability within the context of community. The range of alliances includes social service and government agencies working with the elderly, the incarcerated, and the juvenile populations.

All of the respondents cited the necessity for classes and experiences in specialized areas of concentration outside the currently existing required courses. En L' Aire's "wish list" of supplemental classes grew out of the simple desire to see students exposed to as many forms as possible:

> Tap for its rhythmic focus; Afro-Caribbean for its rich heritage and extraordinary contribution to modern and jazz dance forms; character dance for incredible stamina and coordination building; ballroom for understanding of social periods and partnering techniques; improvisation and conditioning in core classes; Middle Eastern; step dance and other ethnic forms to give breadth and diversity; group drumming; technical theatre (coding file, sec. 0, para 60).

But several respondents perceive specific student deficiencies in other fundamental liberal arts areas, essential items that they consider to be missing from any dancer's "toolbox." Cheval lists "speech, rhetoric, art history, literature" (coding file, sec. 1.2, para 67). Jeté remarks,

> I would also like to see dance programs prepare the dancers in areas other than technique and performance. I know that some do now, but not many . . . things I would have liked to known then, but learned through experience. Here are some ideas: how to prepare a resume or create a promotional video, how to draft a contract, how to write a grant, the importance of promotional materials, the importance of politics, fund-raising, Workman's Compensation, how to do your own tapes . . . people skills (in teaching or soliciting donations), verbal and written articulation, being able to verbally (or in writing) communicate what you want, need or desire to make happen. If you are writing a grant or a press release, you need to know how to write a coherent sentence and spell correctly. A grants panel will look less favorably at a poorly written grant. Also, being able to draft an accurate budget . . . Again, back to the grant writing, if the budget does not make sense, you may not get the funds that you so badly need to support the artistic side of things. So, a speech class, an English class, possibly a business class. The reason for marketing or public relations is that once graduated, you are selling a product—yourself (coding file, sec. 1, para 38 and 59–63).

Barre sums up all of the above: "Knowing how to read and write are the most important skills for any professional" (coding file, sec. 1.2, para 55). Finally, De Chat sees the necessity for experiences outside the curriculum that will stimulate and foster an individual artistic conscience within each student:

> Students need . . . as a spectator and participator [*sic*], an awareness of cultural development both locally and internationally, an exposure to opportunities where society and art intersect . . . artists should not live in a box. Students must stay awake and in open dialogue with cultural and political events that underscore their focus and dedication to a craft . . . not to be insular, not to create in a vacuum (coding file, sec. 0, para 67).

A curriculum must be supported by instruction in order to be effective—if not exemplary. All the respondents cite qualities in outstanding professional educators they believe transcend pedagogical techniques. These characteristics are often observed, sometimes in their own peers' work or when, for instance, a guest artist conducts a master class or potential faculty hire is invited to guest teach a series of classes as part of the interview/ application process. These characteristics include the following:

- The ability to modify technique for safer and more effective training, knowledge of supplemental training, application of class to performances, eye for bringing out potential, emphasis on qualitative aspects of movement (Cheval coding file, sec. 1.4, para 71).
- Connected to the outside world, sensitive and open to listening where students are today, professional backgrounds, participating in the community students are in (Allegro coding file, sec. 0, para 60).
- Honest and caring (Dehors transcript file, p. 3, line 107).
- Analytical skills, empathy, encouragement, daring the student, making sure the student will not settle for the norm, willingness to dialogue with them, urgency for having a student go deeper into the journey for creative fulfillment (De Chat coding file, sec. 0, para 73).

- Teach the desire to learn continually; we can't teach them enough in four years to make them successful, but we can develop habits (Barre transcript file, p. 3, lines 106–108).
- Help students take responsibilities for themselves, their bodies and to open their minds beyond dance class (Barre coding file, sec. 1.13, para 62–63).
- Work well with beginners (Jeté transcript file, p. 6, line 258).
- Attention to detail, generous with time, respect for the art form, high expressive and technical standards, maturity to see the student as a whole (En L' Aire coding file, sec. 0, para 64).

To these educators, effective teaching is inherently holistic and should be ordained always by important personal attributes that deepen instruction and also develop a palpable, nurturing bond with the students.

Skills

Attitude and knowledge, singly or in combination, must be complimented with skills. Respondents attempted to assess the ability of the program to sufficiently prepare the student as a well-rounded, complete package of talent, ability, and potential, ready to enter the dance work force. Additionally, they were asked to consider how the program specifically prepares the student to market him/herself to employers. All respondents strongly stated that their own programs sufficiently provided students with the necessary skills. Each also acknowledged multiple circumstances that challenge the ability to accomplish this. For instance, Barre said, "Not enough faculty" (transcript file, page 3, lines 113–114) and "we need to offer more diverse techniques as well as two semesters of dance history" (transcript file, p. 3, lines 115–116). Jeté at school C is in the position of offering only a departmental minor in dance yet with a very full curriculum—one unusually complete for a secondary interest. The resulting dilemma is that there is still a steady demand for additional dance courses, but if added to the curriculum as it presently stands, this would result in too many credits for a minor yet too few for a major.

Not all programs are able to offer specific courses that prepare students with concrete information and skills needed for the business aspects of a career in the dance field. Unfortunately, among the eight schools there are generally approximately forty to fifty credits required as core curriculum/general education courses. With approximately 120 credits needed to graduate, not all can be dedicated to the student's major field of study. Somehow, compromises must be made as to what is necessary to fulfill the curriculum requirements and still develop career readiness and preparation for the field.

> Many conservatories make beautiful dancers, but they don't know how to read a contract, where to go to find a job, what kinds of promotional materials that may help in the search, the value of networking, or what to put on their resumes (Jeté coding file, sec. 1, para 59).

An exception to this statement comes from Allegro at one of the smaller institutions, school B, who is able to

> devote an entire course for preparing the graduating students, getting their resumes ready, getting some videos ready. I think that it is a big job and that it should be an ongoing job over the four years that they are here (coding file, sec. 0, para 69).

Cheval noted at school H a special career seminar that brought in lecturers that had been professionals. De Chat at school G is comfortable with one-to-one coaching. "We prepare students for choices and realities. The teachers have the necessary range of sensibilities" (transcript file, p. 4, lines 146–147). Similarly, at school D, Barre relies on " the two of us . . . we work with students to discover their desires" (coding file, sec. 1.2, para 69).

School A, the largest in the study, underwent an extensive reform of its program over a three-year period. In the planning phase, the institution apparently did not account for the launching into the job market of a large number of students with such diverse strengths. Sissonne describes this situation:

> We don't have a course or seminar in career planning. That falls into the role of the advisor. We are still visiting (in our revision) the role of the advisor and how that takes place. We are a commuter university. Most of our students are a little older and a little more self-sufficient. Most of them work or teach already in public schools or after-school programs . . . or teaching some kind of body work, etc. I think somatics is a great idea. It gets back to the ideas of what you are going to offer. In the best of all worlds, if advisors are really well-trained, then we could provide that kind of mentorship for students. I do my best to

help them figure out the options, but students need to have their own ideas (transcript file, p. 6, lines 241–249).

Commenting on arts advocacy as initially missing in her own skill set, Jeté encourages her own students to become involved in grass roots political efforts as they consider careers.

> Here in our state, we have many organizations that promote the Arts, give legislative updates, do block bookings, set state standards in education in the arts, and hold conferences. These all directly or indirectly impact the field . . . cuts at the Arts Council in the state and federal levels can impact the amount you can expect in support . . . as much as we like to think we are 'above' politics, it is necessary to do so [participate in arts advocacy] in order to survive" (transcript, p. 8, lines 360–366).

Such participation also affords students exposure to opportunities for future employment or volunteerism in nonperformance related aspects of dance.

Students in some programs firmly believe that they will have a performance career. Others believe that they will attend graduate school in order to eventually teach at the college/university level. Some believe they can successfully pursue and achieve both aspirations. In counseling students, Sissonne is mindful of the dilemma of walking or straddling the line between the respective skill sets required by both the artistic and academic worlds.

> I was trying to maintain my professional career and I actually struggled with two degrees that were offered to me—a PhD and a doctorate of arts. Nobody knows the doctorate of arts. What does that mean? That program was developed for professionals to bring their professional work and experience into that degree. It was a crisis I went through . . . switching back between the programs because I thought the PhD had more prestige but I didn't want to leave my profession. I'm a dancer first and an academic second. I ended up doing the doctorate of arts and I still have thoughts every once in a while, of 'well, that really says what I am' and other times when nobody really knows what the degree is. I have never wanted to take my foot out of either world . . . I thought that a doctorate would be a way to be competitive in a university and to support myself. This has been good to me because I love being in a university most of the time (transcript file, p. 4, lines 163–168).

Behavior

What are the outcomes for students who graduate from the dance program? Did the background, attitude, knowledge, and skills lead to a vocation or avocation anywhere within the spectrum of professional opportunities in the field of dance? As this is a qualitative study, statistical information was not solicited. Rather, the respondents described their perceptions of their own institutions' abilities to successfully facilitate entry into careers or ancillary career paths. What types of dance-related careers are students securing after graduation? How can the programs adapt to the realities of finding a job in today's marketplace?

All respondents again expressed satisfaction with the achievements of their respective programs. Each with pride describes the unique imprint or signature of the program that students carry with them out into new worlds. It may not be an overstatement to characterize this perception in terms of legacy.

This said, several respondents noted that they are cautious not to inadvertently guarantee students that excellence or accomplishment within the halls and studios of academia is an assurance of successfully beginning a career. En L' Aire states that she advises them "to have a back-up plan that allows a lifestyle with dance, yet not as a career" (coding file, sec. 0, para 91). Cheval concurs, "I also encourage them to weigh their love of dance against the competitive and sometimes disheartening realities of the profession" (coding file, sec. 104, para 106). Contrary to active encouragement, De Chat intentionally chooses detachment as a strategy. "I say little unless they take the initiative to come to me. The drive must be realized by the student, not prompted by the teacher" (coding file, sec. 0, para 106). Jeté also deliberately maintains an objective distance, remarking, "I don't do much cheerleading. You either are a dancer or you are not . . . too many questions and risks" (coding file, sec. 1, para 94). None of the respondents refers to ever speaking directly with parents in discussing student plans beyond graduation.

But institutions themselves must hold realistic expectations for their capacity to prepare students as well as for the promises they make.

> A conservatory, I believe, has a place and a different mission. I think if a dancer really wants to enter the professional field, then they should go to the BFA . . . I believe conservatories have to update as well, you know, about the changing world. The problem I have is that dance departments have their curriculum designed under the great illusion

that their students are going to become professional dancers, but when you look at the reality of their graduates, how many really ever become professional dancers? They are training them for some sort of mythical thing (Sissonne transcript file, p. 4, lines 156–161).

For the student now newly armed with a liberal arts degree, an institution typically offers and provides assistance in finding employment through the campus career placement office. But with the exception of En L' Aire, respondents feel that these services are virtually nonexistent for graduating dance students. This is not a major issue for Allegro, who feels that "for dancers, it's being in the right place at the right time. Faculty connections help" (coding file, sec. 0, para 78). The dissatisfaction can be deeply felt: "The Office of Career Services is great for just about everyone except performing arts according to students. Students go to faculty for this" (Jeté transcript file, p. 7, lines 316–317). Barre states, "No one on campus understands dance or has any desire to learn. I do all the individual work with students. I get no answers from the career office as to why it doesn't help" (transcript file, p. 4, lines 135–136). Cheval says that at school H, there was "no contact with the career placement office. All support came from within the dance department" (transcript file, p. 5, lines 202–203). Sissonne, from school A, specifically would not comment on this question.

There is also frustration pertaining to marketing of the programs to attract potentially new students. The findings in this study show that relationships between the programs and the admissions offices are also tenuous at best. Allegro seems to have the most cooperative situation, stating, "We have nice facilities and a strong program. It's not that important, but I have worked with the admissions office to beef up ideas" (transcript file, p. 3, lines 109–110). Sissonne, from school A, says, "I can't touch on that" (transcript file, p. 6, line 240) and "Poor" (transcript file, p. 3, line 101). Barre from school D (at where the program closed in May 2003), describes her experience:

Fair, now nil due to closure of the program . . . the department always had to do the aggressive marketing. We have done all the follow-up work. It is remarkable that we had a program at all (transcript file, p. 4, lines 129–136) . . . poor, badly produced brochures due to lack of time and talent, possibly money. It has been six years since the last new brochure. The last brochure that came out for the new football program is in beautiful color and is obviously very expensive . . . We

were able to submit a copy, but editing and layout was done by some-
one else (transcript file, p. 3, lines 101–104).

But Jeté at school C explains an ironically fortuitous dilemma: "One
challenge is that the dance program is buried in the department of Communication Arts! The department does the best promotion . . . now classes
are overloaded, so it would be a disservice to promote more heavily"
(transcript file, p. 7, line 303–306).

Summary

Aside from the National Association of Schools of Dance accreditation
standards, a professional, peer-generated rubric for dance career readiness and preparation has yet to be developed or implemented. Accord-
ingly, this study posed a research question to provide an opportunity for
the respondents to engage in thought and reflection pertaining to how
their individual programs prepare their students for career paths in dance.
The participants provided both information and opinion about the principles and practices that they employ in implementing their undergraduate degree programs.

Five categories of consideration were used to organize questions and
data. This model enabled the researcher to identify parallels, contrasts,
and comparisons within the results. The data shows that a common goal
is found in striving to maintain the integrity of attitude, knowledge, skills,
and behavior within the overall institutional identity, which itself may or
may not be able to keep pace with ever-evolving issues in the field of
dance.

The phenomenological nature of this study allowed the participants
to address topics through a mechanism independent of—and often in spite
of—their own institutional cultures. In doing so, they revealed concerns
over recognition and perception of their programs. These programs often exist autonomously, if not in a vacuum, from the institution as a
whole. The ideas and experiences raised by these educators are clearly
addressed daily simply through the carrying out of their individual responsibilities but are often not voiced or able to be voiced outside of their
departments. Clearly the research question itself strikes at core issues for
these educators—acceptance, stability, and longevity of programs that
claim to sufficiently prepare students for careers in dance. Chapter 5 will
interpret the results of the findings.

Chapter Five

Results and Conclusions

Introduction

Because the marketplace for professional careers in dance has expanded in ways never envisioned by Colby, Larsen, H'Doubler, and their students (see chapter 2), educators and researchers responsible for accreditation and policy development in postsecondary dance programs have recognized the necessity for renewed and attentive dialogue, representing a continuum of concerns as to the health of the art form in America and the significance of the art form in university settings. Because there is a symbiotic relationship between the art form, higher education, and American society at large, the issues to be explored must focus on how to best serve both the separate and collective needs of these populations.

The purpose of this investigation was for the researcher and participants to analyze the circumstances, situations, and activities that are involved in dance education. In determining the most effective principles and practices in preparing students for careers, the researcher and participants acquired new clarity regarding the physical and social contexts for these phenomena. Both the process of participating as well as the findings themselves can now be applied to the work they do at their institutions and to the field at large.

The phenomenological design of this study afforded the necessary for looking within individual cases. This enabled each participant's answers to create a specific snapshot of his/her institution. Entering this study with no preconceived theory on the part of this researcher or the participants, it also became very apparent, however, that the respondents' collective answers provided clear evidence that effective principles and practices cross the contextual lines of the five categories of questions. Indeed, commonalities on both the successes as well as the serious issues shared among the institutions in the study constituted a zeitgeist of the entire field. This implied a rubric for dance career preparation comprised of nine themes that encapsulate what the respondents consider to be the most essential principles and practices necessary for successful programs.

Implications of the Study

From the data this researcher has determined that there are nine principles and practices, which when taken collectively constitute the concerns of the dance educators in this study as they consider their abilities to justify the continuation and/or expansion of the programs at their institutions. Although principles are understood as fundamental values or truths and practices as the execution of these, the terms are used by the researcher in tandem. However, because the nine principles and practices are not necessarily operational in tandem at any given school in this study, this researcher has described them collectively as goals, which can contribute to an ideal program.

These nine principles and practices are not represented as progressing in a consecutive or progressive sequence. Nonetheless, influences on each other or cause-and-effect relationships between or among them might be drawn. In this chapter, individual explanations of each will be provided, mindful of the relatedness of each concept to the others.

1. Creating Consciousness of the Transnational and Global Context of Dance

Consciousness of the cross-cultural context for dance and its implications for dance programs in the twenty-first century is highly influenced by the performance backgrounds of the participants. Listing extensive and impressive collaborations with international artists, the individual resumes of the respondents read like a "who's who" of choreographers and companies from around the world.

Those participants most passionate in embracing of intercultural consciousness in their program are those who identify a key experience with an influential figure of ethnic or cultural identity different from the respondent. Citing specific dancers and choreographers as having had major

xperiences form a canon of pedagogy, history, and experiences. Many
astitutions de-emphasize the importance of advanced degrees in order to
acrease the ability of fine arts departments in identifying candidates with
ae strongest artistic talents and experiences. Often these individuals are
mployed as visiting artists in residence. The issue becomes whether or
ot the school is willing to apply this hiring practice to the core faculty so
aat ultimately the quality and reputation of the program and department
based upon the talents of these full-time personnel.

The participant's responses tell us of the professional performance
ad choreographic experiences that comprise impressive and extensive
gs of the respondents' journeys to their current positions. Herein lies
a opportunity for an institution to enhance opportunities for faculty sup-
ort and development. Providing additional financial compensation to
xperienced faculty to mentor artists in residence (or other untenured
culty members in a dance department) needs to be explored in order to
ovide to the entire department the enrichment and benefit that such a
actice affords. This can be particularly useful within the field of dance
ae to large numbers of untenured faculty traversing and attempting to
nction in both the academic and artistic worlds.

Personal sense of security and longevity in one's position also affects
e quality of individual and collective morale. Unfortunately, that secu-
y is partially a function of a well-informed employer who supposedly
as a comprehension and appreciation of the completeness of each
orker's craft and individual responsibilities. The lack of administrative
miliarity with dance in all its aspects is therefore a serious issue for
nce faculty.

Respondents appear to simply "make do" with institutional practices
this arena rather than to become proactive for change. While the pro-
am at school C is stable at present, a new incoming dean has yet to
esent his/her view of the arts or departmental support, budget, or sur-
al. The respondents at school A, overworked and exhausted, simply
e with the reality that their school does not recognize the arts. This
ults in cynicism and anger at institutional politics. It would appear that
ch individual negotiates his/her own coping system in lieu of enhance-
nts coming from the administration.

influences on their careers, respondents were encouraged and inspired to look at dance from a very broad, global perspectives as performers and intellectually to appreciate dance in international and Native American cultures, grounding them at the beginning of their careers with broad views of "what dance is." These early influences have since manifested vision and leadership initiative for integrating dance and the intercultural community.

Creating this individual consciousness was a process of assimilation of sensibility from mentoring figures or circumstances. However at an institutional level, such evolution of thought and transformation of perspective cannot be enforced through administrative mandate no matter how "politically correct," but can be achieved through a process of osmosis that includes dialogue, study, and experience.

2. Honoring the Multicultural Fabric of American Dance

In this country, the presence of a monocultural, Eurocentric bias in higher education dance programs is inconsistent with the larger movement toward multicultural literacy across the structures of overall American educational reform. The results of the study show that inclusion and application of this perspective is missing in dance history, dance appreciation, criticism, aesthetics, philosophy, composition, and technique classes. Correction of this omission is not only central to maintaining integrity in the field of postsecondary dance education but is vital to building a context for broadening the audience base in an increasingly diverse American society.

Afrocentric presence in the dance programs is specifically not acknowledged by seven out of the eight schools in this study. This is consistent with the use of inclusive but broad wording of the values of identity and mission for each school as well as in minimal curriculum.

It is consistent with the frequent generalization that in the arts, people merely "play" that some institutions may not ever go further and engage in deeper questions of African American presence in the dance curriculum itself. This situation particularly pertains to school C, a Methodist-affiliated school in an isolated area of rural America with a large Mennonite religious population and therefore very culturally removed from African American presence as well. It should also be noted that school D is also Methodist affiliated and located in an original confederate state with a city that is considered to be the home of the modern-day civil rights movement in America. This institution, too, does not engage in questions of African American presence in its dance program.

School B, a four-year college of the Evangelical Lutheran Church of America, described itself in its mission statement as rooted in the Christian gospel and incorporating a global perspective. It might be noted that school B with its long-standing Norwegian heritage is an institution that held a long-standing prohibition against social dancing at the college, and in 1915, a faculty decision was made to include dancing among the forbidden amusements. The student newspaper in early 1961 conducted a poll indicating that two out of three students would rather not room with a "Negro," over half would not dance with a "Negro," and only one out of three would invite a "Negro" to church on campus. Now courses in world traditions are offered as well as one in diversity issues for teaching students who will work with children in multicultural settings.

Intentionally addressing how to build institutional consensus for honoring the multicultural fabric in American, dance is now a common practice for many schools. Previously, these schools followed the pattern of prioritizing European American training and aesthetics because the majority of the faculty was trained only in this area. Typically, no full-time faculty are specialists in dance styles representative of African, Latin American, and Caribbean dance. If offered at all, these are taught by adjuncts in the community and remain peripheral to the core curriculum.

Honoring the multicultural fabric in American dance is an issue approached by selected schools in the study although there are no mandates or even national postsecondary recommendations to guide them. For school A, it is essentially a "nonissue." For school B, it is addressed through enrichment and exposure. For school C, it is embedded in curriculum and instruction guided by vision. The implications are that institutions are left to their own devices to acknowledge and address this issue.

3. Broadening Leadership Potential and Capacity in Academic Dance Administration

Dimensions of general administrative areas of responsibility in dance in higher education include functioning variously in the roles of artist, communicator, educator, facilitator, motivator, planner, resource developer, fund-raiser, public relations manager, arts advocate, scholar, mentor, and visionary leader. Specialization in these areas requires competency training in the principles, practices, tasks, and responsibilities unique to

dance administration, particularly in order to meet the dem
needs of dance programs as they expand the range of nev
portunities for graduating students to be employed in no
career trajectories. Only two respondents considered them
been prepared for the administrative responsibilities requi
their current positions.

Among the schools in this study, it is apparent that bro
ership potential in dance administration is a concept witl
nated effort generated from within the postsecondary fie
nondegreed "artists turned administrators" become so by
of default and on-the-job training. One important resour
for these "baptism by fire" individuals is participation i
organizations.

It is ironic that while the respondents in this study lea
of administration as capably as possible—simply by experie
of training programs in arts management and administrati
oped in the 1990s that continue now to equip a new genera
students to be the next young managers of cultural and e
programs, including dance. Leadership potential and capaci
as a result.

4. Enhancing Opportunities for Faculty Suppc Development, and Advancement

Between "bleak" and "wonderful," the study results inclu
of faculty views pertaining to their current employment s
tionally, dance educators also assess their overall career
of going with the current, treading water, or swimming
respondents seem to feel that their own abilities to prepar
integrity is influenced by whether or not there is a ser
institutional support provided by the institution for nurtu
vidually as valued core faculty. They see a lack of satisf
ties for ongoing professional support, development, an
unless these opportunities are self-initiated from within t

Contributing to this situation is the fact that dance is a
accredited discipline in higher education. As such, there
tradition of principles and practices across this subject a
upon which entire departments can draw. Nor is there a
men and women who have taught within this field in a

5. Fostering Synergy and Interdisciplinary Collaboration within the Institution

It would appear from the study that collaborations occur most frequently as project-specific activities. These projects tend to be product oriented and geared toward performance outcomes. But if dance educators were to expand curricular objectives to also include reaching the general student population, a different synergy would be generated.

Inherent in dance education is an exploration of kinesthetic intelligence—which itself develops the other (previously six and now) seven of Gardner's intelligences. Therefore, movement classes could be designed to challenge students with assignments in traditionally cognitive modalities of learning such as sequencing, spatial reasoning, linguistic association, and grouping. Additionally, because dance and movement training is largely based through developing a sense of ensemble among the participants, the skills of team building, negotiation, and conflict resolution easily applies to students of business management, psychology, and social sciences. Are dance educators willing to explore this application of their bodily/kinesthetic body of information to a broadening of curricular offerings to a generalist community of students?

Ongoing interdisciplinary partnerships between departments offer the potential for a continuous reciprocal exchange of creative energy and inspiration. Only school A, via its Dance within Disciplines program, has developed and sustained a high level of interdepartmental as well as intercollegiate cooperation. As a replicable model, it is likely that other institutions would benefit from borrowing and building upon the mechanisms devised by school A to develop within their own campuses positive and successful collaborative outcomes.

Dismantling dance programs may require breaking down walls between disciplines and the university to become cooperative partners. Coming from the top down, administrative support would signal to these respondents a palpable and unusual fostering of synergy.

6. Fostering Synergy and Alliances between the Institution and Community

Despite the fact that we know that historically dance has served in encoding religious, social, and political values for a culture as well as contributing to social solidarity in daily life, the primary purpose of dance education in America has evolved to either prepare students for professional careers or to provide broader training within a liberal arts context. However, according to a 1997 *American Canvas* report published by the National Endowment for the Arts, too often arts institutions are elitist, racially segregated, class based, and isolated from the communities they claim to serve but do not.

Outreach work (not to be confused with field practicum or student teaching, as is the frequently the case) is not a priority for the majority of programs in this study. Outreach efforts for most of the schools are add-ons at best. Performance opportunities range from main stage productions to off-campus events at school B. School H dancers conduct lecture/demonstrations at local schools.

School C faces local misconceptions imbedded within the homogenous rural community in which the institution is located creating an obstacle to developing synergy and alliance. But despite preconceived ideas within the large Mennonite population that a woman cannot achieve more than a high school or community college degree nor consider dance a viable career option, could that not provide incentive to actively initiate innovative ways to build bridges of partnership?

Cutting-edge curricular reform resulting in positive and dynamic synergy with the community grows out of consensus reached under effective leadership. In the case of school A, this leadership is driven by the vision of Sissonne, who deserves significant credit for facilitating the institution's commitment to bridging education and the community. This vision required a sweeping evaluation process and reformulation of the dance department's mission and identity, a "buy-in" to the alliance by community partners and funding to underwrite the initiative.

To similarly accomplish such reform within other schools, especially smaller or geographically diverse ones, could appear to be daunting if not impossible. However, a key component of the program design in school A's initiative is replicability. As a "living laboratory," school A intends to serve as a national model, generously offering technical assistance to other schools in service to the field.

7. Promoting Holistic, Integrated Pedagogy, and Practice

With the exception of school D, it appears that the participants in the study find themselves "taking inventory" in an ongoing way. What can realistically be accomplished to "form" a dancer in four undergraduate years and two to four years at the graduate levels? The guiding concepts and underlying suppositions in pedagogy must include application of the artistic process itself. However, in an institutional setting, the result can be a training approach that is compartmentalized rather than integrated. The challenge for administrators and faculty is to find a healthy counterpoint among the many technical, choreographic, performing, historical, and critical aspects of the discipline in order to best serve students who are anticipating careers in a richly diverse and "real" professional dance world.

Again, with the exception of school D, each institution in the study is actively working to integrate and regularly update aspects of kinesiology, anatomy, fitness, and nutrition into course content in order to create balance with the mental and physical demands that come with relentless hours of technique classes. Because the training of a dancer involves cultivating healthy mental/emotional connections to technique, the pedagogical antennae must be finely tuned to addressing deficiencies in personal habits or nonuseful personal values. This does not appear to present a challenge to the schools that only stand to gain in credibility by staying current with the latest information and practices in all holistic areas.

8. Insuring the Integrity of Readiness for Performance Careers

The question of whether college dance can be of service to the professional performance world through providing adequately trained talent remains open to myriad responses. How students and parents imagine the careers in dance and how faculty and working professionals experience and communicate the realities of "the business" are often two very different paradigms. Bridging the gap of information and understanding is a major responsibility facing administrators and faculty charged with designing a curriculum designed to develop a student who is able to enter the job market. A background beyond excellence in dance training is necessary. The commercial and nonprofit performance worlds have well-earned reputations for being impersonal and insensitive to the needs of young, new talent trying to break into the field. To venture into this arena in which the "cattle call" audition process is the norm is to step away from the nurturing environment of the academic dance setting or the atmosphere of exploration and discovery that serve the artistic missions of many nonprofit ballet and modern dance companies. The respondents in the study all counsel their students that a performance career is a gamble and that one cannot go into the field "starry eyed."

The integrity of readiness for performance careers requires comprehensively training students for the marketplace but must also fairly, adequately, and realistically prepare them to anticipate the often-overwhelming realities of "the business." Therefore, it is incumbent on the program—while making no claims to or guarantees of "getting that big break"—to honestly ask whether it is truly offering all the resources possible to fairly send its graduates out into a world so vastly different than the institutional environment.

The data in this study does not suggest that schools A, B, or C can realistically offer an integrity of readiness at the present time for career paths in performance.

9. Insuring the Integrity of Readiness for Nonperformance Careers

If one espouses the idea that artistic development, connection, or nourishment can occur offstage as well as onstage with equal validity and reward, then a wider arena of career paths becomes available to students leaving college and university dance programs. Faculty and administration in this study have kept pace with many dance-related fields and developed curricula that prepare students to become marketable in nonperformance areas. These provide options for students who realistically may not possess the necessary talent for jobs as dancer or choreographers as well as for those who become excited at connecting other disciplines to their intrinsic love of the art form. Respondents report on students who are now engaged in professional work as widely ranging as the fields of horticulture, business, fashion, elementary education, and social work while still taking dance classes and sometimes actually incorporating movement activities into their work.

The results of this study indicate that schools A, B, and C all expose students to aspects of dance therapy, technical theater, dance management, dance notation and reconstruction, sports medicine, arts management, dance writing and research, videography for dance, and music for dance. There is integrity in readiness for further study at the graduate level or through internships. There is sufficient exposure but not sufficient integrity of readiness to immediately begin nonperformance careers in the above mentioned areas.

Conclusions

The research topic of this study led to developing categories of questions pertaining to background, attitude, knowledge, skills, and behaviors of students and teachers in the fields of dance education. Eight professional educators representing college/university-level programs responded. Programs at eight corresponding institutions were targeted for specific comparison.

The data results show consensus among the respondents that in 2003, the overall state of dance education as a field is healthy. There is also unanimity of opinion and enthusiastic interest for clarification of and improvement upon current principles and practices. While there is agreement that the elements of technical skill, aesthetic insight, intellectual rigor, and work ethic must be developed in every dance student, the dilemma in this researcher's opinion lies in a lack of consensus around the meaning of "to sufficiently prepare" for career readiness in the twenty-first century. How is "sufficiently" to be defined?

It is imperative, then, that institutions develop programming and studies that reflect every possible career opportunity. In a profession that has experienced expansion in job possibilities beyond the traditional paths of performance, choreography, or teaching at the public school level or in local or private studios, institutions need to widen their horizons.

Because current programs and curricula in secondary institutions were primarily developed before the simultaneous expansion and shrinkage of media and technology in the mid-1990s, present practices have not necessarily kept pace with today's globalization of education and culture. And there is unqualified agreement among the respondents that the impact of this revolution in communications has been felt just as strongly in dance education as in other academic fields. There is further agreement that longevity and survival for dance education in academia will significantly depend upon developing programs that embody and espouse the contextual knowledge of dance within and to serve an increasingly global job market.

Many efforts have already been done to diversify the curriculum. Primarily, these manifest themselves as add-ons or peripheral courses. Doing such, however, does not necessarily link the discipline with culture(s) in a symbiotic way. There is, therefore, an increasing opinion that it is time for dance curriculum to evolve beyond its historic organization into standard and traditional theory and studio classes. Instead, interrelationships should be developed within the discipline, across arts and nonart disciplines, and across cultures. This said, the recurring issue will be whether such a shift in consciousness and practice can also allow for maintaining a "sufficient" foundation of technique in all styles for a student.

Nine institutional goals for achieving "sufficient" preparation for career paths in dance emerged, but it should be pointed out that if one eliminated the first word of each phrase, there is left merely a concept. Restore the initial word to any phrase—creating, honoring, broadening, enhancing, fostering, promoting, ensuring—and the meaning changes, becoming active and action driven. These concepts become goals. From concrete goals, objectives and measurable outcomes can be developed.

This study does not explore nor will it attempt to suggest how the principles and practices might be translated into action in order to achieve the desired results. That work falls to task forces and evaluation teams. But wrapped around the pragmatic considerations of determining whether a program and a student are the right match for each other there must be trust. Therefore, within each institution there must also be a process of constant inventory, reflection, and adjustment in order that the integrity of its principles and practices are always maintained.

Suggestions for Future Research

This study raised new ideas and concerns that fell outside the parameters of the research question. The results of this research suggest that there are many aspects of postsecondary dance education that warrant inquiry and investigation for the first time. Future research into the following topic areas could contribute to a more comprehensive understanding of the increasingly sophisticated role that dance plays in American culture and education:

- A new comprehensive survey similar to the 1955 study cited by Ingram to determine how dance programs are placed into the structures or hierarchies of physical education, fine arts, or communications departments.
- A quantitative survey of BA and BFA standards among the three hundred American colleges and universities that offer dance as a major.

- A study of programs that incorporate fitness, nutrition, somatics, kinesiology, and technology as core curriculum.
- Investigation of the relationship between preparations of postsecondary students to teach dance in K–12 settings with the increasing elimination of the arts from public school education. Future development of university dance programs will depend upon confidence that a steady flow of talented young people will continue to flow through the audition and admissions door. From where or whence will these students come?
- Investigation of the relationship and interactions between dance departments and their parent institutions in initiating dialogue and programming pertaining to multicultural and global awareness.
- A follow-up study that again poses this researcher's investigative question, this time to graduates of dance degree programs as well as to producers from the commercial sector, artistic directors from the nonprofit sector, and human resource managers in the related nonperformance fields.
- Individual studies of the nonperformance related fields such as dance notation and reconstruction, sports medicine, dance therapy, arts management, dance videography, etc.

Additionally, there is no doubt in this researcher's mind that readers of this study will ascertain further areas worthy of research, and they are encouraged to do so.

Summary

The principles and practices emerging from the respondents' statements as well as the areas in which further research might be of benefit to this field point this researcher to one overriding new awareness that within the research question itself as well as the respondents' observations lies an implied assumption as to the very meaning of the word "professional." No definition was put forth by the researcher in the event that it might impose a bias or inhibit freely given responses. Yet no questions were ever raised by the participants as to the meaning or connotations for this term. Nonetheless, in the fields of dance and dance education, artists, educators, administrators, parents, advocates, and others are linked—if not conjoined—by an understanding that this discipline manifests itself in either professional or nonprofessional form.

The extraordinary evolution of this discipline in America and the world in the last one hundred years has matured this vibrant art form to its most advanced levels of meaning and accessibility. But with the new sophistication of dance as well as the teaching of dance has also come a complexity of perception that may require a new interpretation of what is meant when describing a "dance professional."

Is a scholarly reexamination of the fundamental roots of this discipline in order? Or is such an inquiry, because it ultimately raises spiritual and humanistic questions, in fact inevitable? Who are the arbiters, spokespersons, or high priests of meaning for dance in a global twenty-first century?

It is clear that the field of dance education in America in 2003 is poised to demonstrate, for the first time, that movement is basic, relevant, and is a social construct of all human experience and can intentionally be employed to join and unite disciplines and cultures. What will be required first is a unified and fortified commitment by dance educators and institutions to take hands together and begin that journey of transformation.

References

Abrams, G. L. (1991). Student as teacher, teacher as student [Monograph]. *Focus on Dance, XII*, 80-83.

Anderson, J. (1977). *Ballet and modern dance*. Princeton, NJ: Princeton Books.

Arbeau, T. (1589). *Orchesography*. Quoted in Horst, 7.

Babbie, E. (1990). *Survey research methods*. Belmont, CA: Wadsworth Publishing.

Babbie, E. (1998). *The practice of social research* (8th Ed.). Belmont, CA: Wadsworth Publishing.

Barranger, M. (1994). *Understanding plays*. Boston, MA: Allyn and Bacon.

Beckford, R. (1979). *Katherine dunham*. New York: Marcel Decker, Inc.

Beiswanger, B. P. (1960). National section on dance, its first ten years. *Journal of Health, Physical Education, and Recreation*, 23.

Berg, B.L. (1998). *Qualitative research methods for the social sciences*. Needham, MA: Allyn & Bacon.

Bockris, V. (1997). *Warhol*. New York: DaCapo Press.

Booth, E. (1997). *The everyday work of art*. Naperville, CA: Sourcebooks, Inc.

Bozza, A. (2002, July 4-14). Eminem: The rolling stone interview. *Rolling Stone Magazine*, 899/900.

Bloom, B. S. (1985). *Developing talent in young people*. New York: Ballantine Books.

Bogdan, R. & Bilken, S. (1982). *Qualitative research for education: An introduction to theory and methods*. Boston, MA: Allyn and Bacon.

Boling, B. (2000). *A dancer's manual: A motivational guide to professional dancing*. Taluca Lake, CA: Rafter Publishing.

Brockett, O. (2003). *History of the theatre* (9th Ed.). Boston, MA: Allyn and Bacon.

Brown, J. M. (1979). *The vision of modern dance*. Princeton, NJ: Princeton Books.

Buckle, R. (1988). *George balanchine, ballet master*. New York: Random House Publishers.

Clemente, K. (1991). Dance education degree programs in colleges and universities [Monograph]. *Focus on Dance, XII*, 41-46.

Cleveland, W. (2000). *Art in other places*. Westport, CT: Praeger.

Cohen, R. (2003). *Acting on* (4th Ed.). Boston, MA: MacGraw-Hill Publishers.

Consortium of National Arts Education Associations, International Council of Fine Arts Deans, & Council of Arts Accrediting Associations (2001). *To move forward: An affirmation of continuing commitment to arts education*. Retrieved October 23, 2002 from http://www.naea-reston.org/ToMove.pdf.

Crawford, J. R. (1987). Dance MATERIAL (dance, music, and art training and education resulting in aesthetic literacy) [Monograph]. *Focus on Dance, XII*, 64-71.

Creswell, J. (1994). *Research design: Qualitative and quantitative approaches*. Thousand Oaks, CA: Sage Publications.

D'Amboise, J., Cooke, H. & George, C. (1983). *Teaching the magic of dance*. New York: Simon & Schuster.

De Mille, A. (1961). *The book of the dance*. New York: Golden Press.

Dimondstein, G. (1971). *Children dance in the classroom*. New York: The Macmillan Company.

DuPont, B. (1977). *Dance: The art of production*. Saint Louis: C.V. Mosby Company.

Eckert, J. (2003). *Harnessing the wind*. Champaign, IL: Human Kinetics.

Ellfeldt, L. (1976). *Dance from magic to art*. Dubuque, IA: Wm. C. Brown Company

Ferdun, E. (1990). *Moving dance: poetics and praxis*. Reston: National Dance Association Dance Scholar Lecture.

Firestone, W. (1987). Meaning in method: the rhetoric of quantitative and qualitative research. *Educational Researcher*, 16(7), 16-21.

Fischer, J. (1988). *Real christians don't dance*. Omaha, NE: Word Publishing.

Flinn, D. (1997). *Musical! A grand tour*. New York: Schirmer Books.

Fowler, C. & Little, A. (1977). *Dance as education*. Washington, D.C.: National Dance Association and Alliance for Arts Education.

Fowler, F. J. (1993). *Survey research methods*. Newbury Park, CA; Sage.

Fraenkel, J. & Wallen, N. (1996). *How to design and evaluate research in education*. New York: McGraw Hill.

Franklin, E. (1996). *Dance imagery*. Champaign, IL: Human Kinetics.

Gardner, H. (1983). *Frames of mind: A theory of multiple intelligences*. New York: Basic Books.

Garfunkel, T. (1994). *On wings of joy*. New York: Little, Brown and Company.

Gibbons, B. (1991). A prismatic approach to analysis of style in dance as a paradigm for dance education. [Monograph]. *Focus on Dance, XII*, 12-17.

Grant, G. (1982). *Technique manual and dictionary of classical ballet*. New York: Dover Publications.

Grein, J.T. (1908, March 3). The palace: A new dancer". *The New York Times*. Retrieved April 16, 2003, from http://www.nytimes.com

Grody, S. (1996). *Conversations with choreographers*. Portsmouth, NH: Heinemann Press.

Guba, E. & Lincoln, Y. (1988). Do inquiry paradigms imply inquiry methodologies? In D. M. Fetterman (Ed.) *Qualitative approaches to evaluation in education* (89-115). New York: Praeger.

Hagood, T. K. (2000). Traditions and experiment/diversity and change: Issues for dance in american education. *Arts Education Policy Review*. July, 101(6), 21-28.

Hall, F. (1972). *The world of ballet and dance*. New York: Hamlyn Publishing.

Hammond, S. (1982). *Ballet: Beyond the basics*. Mountain View, CA: Mayfield Press.

Hanna, J. (1999). *Partnering dance and education*. Champaign, IL: Human Kinetics.

Hayes, E. (1977). Dance in the universities: Yesterday, today, and tomorrow. *Arts in Society*. 13(2), 3405-5.

H'Doubler, M. (1927). *The dance and its place in education*. New York: Harcourt, Brace and Co.

H'Doubler, M. (1940). *Dance: A creative art experience*. New York: F.S. Crofts & Co.

Hodes, S. (1998). *A map of making dances*. New York: Ardsley House Publishers.

Horosko, M. (1997, March). Options in paying tuition. *Dance Magazine*, 71(3), 100-102.

Horst, L. (1979). *Pre-classic dance forms*. New York: Dance Horizons Publications.

Howe, E. C. (1937). What business has modern dance in physical education? *Journal of Health and Physical Education*, 132.

Idhe, D. (1986). *Experimental phenomenology: An introduction*. Albany, NY: State University of New York Press.

Ingram, A. (1986). Philosophical discussion of where dance belongs in higher education [Monograph]. *Dance: The Study of Dance and the Place of Dance in Society*. 194-203.

Johnson, B. & Christensen, L. (2000). *Educational research; Qualitative and quantitative approaches*. Boston, MA: Allyn and Bacon.

Keali'inohomoku, J. (1992). *Dancing by gerald jones*. New York: Harry N. Abrams.

Kerr, J. A. (1992). Afro centric forms in 20th century american dance history: Transforming course content and the curriculum [Monograph]. *Focus on Dance, XII*, 53-63.

Kirstein, L. (1942). *The book of the dance*. New York: Garden City Publishing Co.

Knobler, N. (1971). *The visual dialogue*. New York: Holt, Rinehart, and Winston.

Kraines, M. (2001). *Jump into jazz*. Mountain View, CA: Mayfield Publishing Co.

Kraus, R. (1969). *History of the dance*. Englewood Cliffs, NJ: Prentice Hall Publishers.

Kraus, R. & Chapman, S. (1997). *History of the dance in art and education* (3rd Ed.). Boston, MA: Allyn and Bacon.

Laban, R. (1948). *Modern educational dance*. London: MacDonald and Evans.

Laban, R. (1971). *The mastery of movement* (3rd Ed.). Boston, MA: Plays, Inc.

Land, B. (2002). *History of dance and culture* (2nd Ed.). Boston, MA: Pearson Custom Publishing Co.

Larson, J. (1997). *Rent*. New York; William Morrow Publishers.

Lee, C. (1987). *An introduction to classical ballet*. New Jersey; Erlbaum Associates.

Lincoln, Y. S., & Guba, E. G. (1985). *Naturalistic inquiry*. Beverly Hills, CA: Sage.

Lloyd, M. in Rorek, T. (1972). The connecticut college american dance festival. *Dance Perspectives*, 50, 10.

Locke, L., Spirduso, W. & Silverman, S. (1993). *Proposals that work* (3rd Ed.*): A guide for planning dissertations and grant proposals*. Newbury Park, CA: Sage.

Long, R. (1995). *The black tradition in american dance*. New York: Smithmark Publishers.

MacLaren, W. H. (1980). The deceased other: Presence and absence [Abstract]. *Dissertation Abstracts*, 41(6-B), 2332.

Maletic, V. (1987). *Body-space-expression*. Berlin: Mouton de Gruyter.

Martin, J. (1952). *World book of modern ballet*. Cleveland: World Publishing.

Maxwell, J. (1996). *Qualitative research design*. Thousand Oaks, CA: Sage.

Mazo, J. (1977). *Prime movers: The makers of modern dance in america*. Princeton, NJ: Princeton Books.

McCracken, G. (1988). *The long interview*. Newbury Park, CA: Sage.

McDonagh, D. (1986). *Dance: A very social history*. New York: Rizzoli International Publications.

McMahon, P. (2000). *Dancing wheels*. Boston: Houghton Mifflin.

Merriam, S. (1988). *Case study research in education: A qualitative approach*. San Francisco: Jossey-Bass.

Miles, M. & Huberman, A. (1994). *Qualitative data analysis: An expanded sourcebook* (2nd Ed.). Thousand Oaks, CA: Sage.

Minton, S. (1997). *Choreography*. Champaign, IL: Human Kinetics.

Minton, S. (2003). *Dance: Mind and body*. Champaign, IL: Human Kinetics.

Mirault, D. (1994). *Dancing for a living*. Taluca Lake, CA: Rafter Publishing.

Mirault, D. (1998). *Dancing for a living –2*. Taluca Lake, CA: Rafter Publishing.

Murphy, S. (1986). Why dance? A functional perspective [Monograph]. *Dance: The Study of Dance and the Place of Dance in Society*, 93-99.

National Endowment for the Arts. (2002). *Learning through the arts; A guide to the national endowment for the arts*. Retrieved September 21, 2002 from http://nea.gov

Oliver, W. (1992). *Dance in higher education*. Reston, VA: National Dance Association.

Pace, C. R. (1969). In Kraus, R. (1969). *History of the dance*. Englewood Cliffs, NJ: Prentice Hall Publishers.

Patton, M. (1990). *Qualitative evaluation and research methods*. Newbury Park, CA: Sage.

Paul, T. (2003). *So you want to dance on broadway?* Portsmouth, NH: Heineman Publishers.

Penrod, J. (1998). *The dancer prepares*. Irvine, CA: McGraw-Hill, Inc.

Pierce-Boyd, K. (1991). Benign neglect: Issues in mentoring [Monograph]. *Focus on Dance, XII*, 118-123.

Poole, J.A. (1986). Dance for males in education [Monograph]. *Dance: The Study of Dance and the Place of Dance in Society* (174-191).

Pomer, J. (2002). *Perpetual motion*. Champaign, IL: Human Kinetics.

Rorek, T. (1972). The connecticut college american dance festival. *Dance Perspectives*, 50, 10.

Sagolla, L. (1998, November 13). Should dancers go to college? *Backstage*, 30.

Shaw, J. M. (1975). *A history of st. olaf college*. Northfield, MN: The St. Olaf College Press.

Shawn, T. (1960). *One thousand and one night stands*. New York: Doubleday & Co.

Smith-Autard, J. M. (1994). *The art of dance in education*. London: A & C Black, Publishers.

Straus, A. & Corbin, J. (1998). *Basics of qualitative research: Techniques and procedures for developing grounded theory*. Thousand Oaks, CA: Sage.

Tesch, R. (1990). *Qualitative research: Analysis types and software tools*. New York: Falmer.

Todd, M. (1959). *The thinking body*. Hightstown, NJ: Princeton Book Company.

Topaz, M. (1994). Dancers in cap and gown: Some leading california professors discuss what the present and the future hold for dance students. *Dance Magazine*, 68(5).

Van Dyke, J. (1992). *University dance: Some questions* [Monograph]. *Focus on Dance, XII*, 27-32.

Wagner, A. (1997). *Adversaries of dance: From the puritans to the present*. Chicago: University of Chicago Press.

Walker, C. and Walker, P. (1997). Pre-professional dance training policy considerations. *Arts Education Policy Review*, 98(6), 20.

Weisman, E. (1992). Serving a broad dance community in higher education. [Monograph]. *Focus on Dance*, XII, 89-92.

Whiteman, E. F. (1991). Management competencies for dance administrators in higher education [Monograph]. *Focus on Dance, XII*, 114-117.

Wilson, D. C. (1986). Freelancing: The entrepreneurial dance/movement teacher. *Dance: The Study of Dance and the Place of Dance in Society* (93-99).

Wood, C. & Gillis-Kruman, S. (1991). Developing skills in dance: considerations for teaching adult beginners [Monograph]. *Focus on Dance, XII*, 75-79.

Woodward, S. (1999). Oberlin college: Pioneers in ohio. *Dance Magazine*, 73(2), 60-61.

Wosien, M. (1974). *Sacred dance: Encounter with the gods*. New York: Avon Books.

Wright, J. (2003). *Social dance*. Champaign, IL: Human Kinetics.

Appendix A

Informed Consent Form

You have been asked to participate in a research study conducted by Kathleen E. Klein, a doctoral student at Lynn University. The basis of the research project is to develop a comprehensive comparison of three dance curricula in higher education by examining the history, standards, strengths, weaknesses and achievements of three very distinct existing dance degree programs. The research study will span over a twelve-week period. The goal of this study is to develop a rubric that can assist colleges and universities in providing stronger outcomes for students seeking a career path in dance.

The study involves an open-ended questionnaire about your personal and professional experience in the programs as well as questions regarding previous training in other programs. You may also be asked to participate in a follow-up interview to clarify answers and to review for accuracy. The interviews will be taped and recorded to ensure a more precise analysis of information. The total time involved for each participant will not exceed one and one-half hours.

The information you provide will be kept in strict confidence. Transcriptions of the interview will be made and coded with numerical representation to protect your identity. Reports of this research will not include any identifiable data. The results of this study will be published in a doctoral dissertation and possibly a professional journal. Lynn University's institutional review board has authorized access to all materials related to this research.

You have been selected to participate in this research study based upon your knowledge of and/or experience in the subject to be studied. If you choose not to participate or decide at any time during the study that you prefer not to continue in the study, you may do so without negative consequences. Should you withdraw, your data will be eliminated from the study and will be destroyed. If you do participate, your data will be coded to protect your identity and confidentiality and will be kept for a period of five years. At the end of five years, the data will be destroyed. There is no financial remuneration for participating in this study.

A copy of the final analysis will be provided to each participant upon request at the completion of the study. Questions pertaining to any aspect of the study or your involvement therein may be directed to the researcher Kathleen E. Klein at work (561) 803-2428 or home (561) 585-6032. In the event that you have concerns about this project that you do not wish to address with Kathleen Klein, you may call Dr. William Leary, dissertation committee chairman of Lynn University at (561) 237-7089. Two copies of this informed consent form have been provided. Please sign both, indicating that you have read, understood, and agreed to participate in this research study. Please return one copy to the researcher and keep the other for your files.

Name of participant _____ tel.#_____
(please print)

Signature of participant_____ date_____

Kathleen E. Klein, researcher_____ date_____

Appendix B

Interview Guide

Career Readiness and Preparation Criteria in Undergraduate Dance Degree Programs

By Kathleen Klein

Research Question: *What are the effective principles and practices that exist in effective university-level dance programs that sufficiently prepare students for career paths in dance?*

1.

    a. What is your occupation at this time? How long have you been in this capacity?

    b. In your current work, do you generally operate from one base, or do you work in multiple settings?

    c. Tell me the story of how you came to this program/profession/job.

    d. What is/was your main field of interest: performing, teaching, or other?

    e. What are your perceptions of the views toward dance held by any other persons or groups whom you consider to be influential on you?

2.

    a. Can you describe the personal habits, interests, and values, which you believe students need in order to reach their full potential?

    b. How do you currently view your employment situation?

    c. Could you tell me about your aspirations for future development of university dance programs in general?

3.

    a. Can you tell me about your previous training/experience in the dance field prior to working in this particular institution's dance program?

    b. What background do you feel is necessary for a student to begin in this institution's program regardless of the performing or educational emphasis?

    c. What courses and classes do you consider essential in an undergraduate dance program? Why?

    d. What experiences outside of the required curriculum are necessary to prepare for a career in the field of dance regardless of performing or educational emphasis?

    e. Can you describe the qualities of a teacher (or teachers) in your program that has had a specific influence on students' readiness for a career in dance?

4.

    a. Does this program sufficiently prepare the student in dance technique and history? Why or why not?

    b. Does this program sufficiently prepare the student in terms of information pertaining to careers in the field of dance? How or how not?

5.

    a. How would you characterize the marketing of the dance program by this institution's admissions office?

    b. How would you characterize the role of this institution's career placement office in assisting the graduating student in finding employment in the field of dance?

    c. Do you encourage other prospective students to enroll at this institution? Why or why not?

d. Do you encourage current undergraduate dance students to pursue a career in the field? Why or why not?

6. Conclusion

a. Is there anything more that you would like to say?
b. Are there any questions that you would like to ask me?
c. Can you tell me what this interview experience was like for you?
d. Is there anything that I haven't asked you about that would add to my understanding of what you are telling me?
e. Do you feel there is a need for a study of the kind I am conducting? Why or why not?

About the Author

K athleen Klein is the founding director of dance at Palm Beach Atlantic University in West Palm Beach, Florida. For the past thirty years, she has also served as the executive director of Klein Dance Inc., which operated a thriving school for dance, a small alternative performing space, and the Demetrius Klein Dance Company. She has also been active in the training of the school's three hundred students and is well known in South Florida for her ability to reach her student's highest potential through discipline, grace, imagination, and accomplishment. She received all of her professional dance training with a multitude of various artists in New England. She was employed by the School of Hartford Ballet in Connecticut while attending a rigorous teacher training program and dancing a demanding performance schedule. She has an extensive background in dance technique, pointe and partnering, ballet theory, kinesiology, dance history, music theory, and most important for her students, child psychology and pedagogy. Prior to her engagement at Palm Beach Atlantic University, Kathleen ran the dance department for Palm Beach Community College (Lake Worth, Florida) for six years and also taught dance technique and dance history courses at Florida Atlantic University (Boca Raton, Florida). Kathleen completed her PhD in global leadership at Lynn University in 2004. A Phi Kappa Phi member committed to community service, she is a member of Americans for the Arts, the American Association of University Women, the Florida Dance Association, Florida Association of Health, Physical Education, Recreation and Dance, and the Palm Beach County Cultural Council.